TIMELESS OF THE T
 a beginner's guide

CRAIG HAMILTON-PARKER

Hodder & Stoughton

A MEMBER OF THE HODDER HEADLINE GROUP

British Library Cataloguing in Publication Data
A catalogue record for this title is available from The British Library

ISBN 0 340 70483 7

First published 1999
Impression number   10 9 8 7 6 5 4 3 2 1
Year   2003   2002   2001   2000   1999

Copyright © 1999 by Craig Hamilton-Parker

All rights reserved. No part of this publication may be reproduced or transmitted in any form or by any means, electronic or mechanical, including photocopy, recording, or any information storage and retrieval system, without permission in writing from the publisher or under licence from the Copyright Licensing Agency Limited. Further details of such licences (for reprographic reproduction) may be obtained from the Copyright Licensing Agency Limited, of 90 Tottenham Court Road, London W1P 9HE.

Typeset by Transet Ltd, Coventry, England.
Printed in Great Britain for Hodder & Stoughton Educational,
a division of Hodder Headline Plc, 338 Euston Road, London NW1 3BH
by Cox & Wyman.

Contents

Part 1 — Tibetan civilisation and beliefs

Chapter 1 The root of Tibetan civilisation 1

Chapter 2 Tibetan Buddhism 20

Part 2 — Tibetan wisdom's relevance today

Chapter 3 What can the timeless wisdom of Tibet teach us about ourselves? 51

Chapter 4 What can the timeless wisdom of Tibet teach us about human relationships and sexuality? 58

Chapter 5 What can the timeless wisdom of Tibet teach us about children and the family? 69

Chapter 6 What can the timeless wisdom of Tibet teach us about marriage, the home and our friends? 76

Chapter 7 What can the timeless wisdom of Tibet teach us about work and money? 83

Chapter 8 What can the timeless wisdom of Tibet teach us about health? 90

Chapter 9 What can the timeless wisdom of Tibet teach us about the wider environment and the purpose of human life? 101

Further reading 107

Part 1
TIBETAN CIVILISATION AND BELIEFS

Chapter 1
The root of Tibetan civilisation

The legends about the first people of Tibet have an almost Darwinian theme. A fresco at the Samyey Monastery, the earliest Buddhist monastery which was built in the late eighth century, shows how macaque monkeys transformed into human beings to become the Tibetan race. The legends say that before the advent of human beings, Tibet was a place where the ogress (female giant) of the rocks ran amok. Seeing the distress of the living creatures that lived there, the Bodhisattva of Compassion (Avalokiteshvara) transformed into a macaque monkey and mated with the ogress (an emanation of the goddess Tara). Six baby monkeys were born that bred to make 500 monkeys and who, in the course of time, lost their tails and began to speak. Gradually, they evolved into human beings and were, according to legend, the first Tibetans.

The union of Avalokiteshvara and Tara[1] are important symbols for Tibetans. Avalokiteshvara is the mythic Father of the Nation who is said to have reincarnated repeatedly as the kings of Tibet and today is manifesting[2] as the Dalai Lama. His counterpart, Tara

---

[1] These angelic beings are two of four main enlightened 'gods' who oversee the welfare of Tibet: Tara is the lady of Miraculous Activities, Avalokiteshvara is the Lord of Compassion, Manjushri is the Lord of Wisdom and Vajrapani is the Lord of Power.

[2] Avalokiteshvara is believed to manifest himself in countless ways at the same time and, for example, also exists within lamas such as the Karmapa incarnations.

is the omnipresent Mother of the Nation who reappears in many Tibetan stories as an empress, queen and defender of the ruler. When faced with adversity the Tibetans call on her power to help them overcome their difficulties.

According to tradition, the Kongpori Mountain near Tsethang in the Yarlung valley was the spot at which the union of Avalokiteshvara and Tara took place. Inside the three caves on the mountain slopes, archaic Tibetans erected carvings and stone frescoes to mark this sacred and ancient home of their ancestors. In this same valley Rupati, an Indian king who fled over the Himalayas after his defeat in the Mahabharata war, was crowned the first king of Tibet by 12 wise Bön priests in 127 BCE[3]

The primal myths of the birth of men from monkeys may originate from stories and legends that predate Buddhism or have been adapted from Chinese legends and were incorporated into Tibetan legend. This story which finds its first mention in a compilation of the twelfth to the thirteenth century, may be of Chinese inspiration but taken over by the Tibetans to symbolise the civilising influence of Buddhism (i.e. the prostrate ogress symbolises Tibet herself whose inhabitants are described in the Chinese texts as 'red faced demons, eaters of raw flesh and drinkers of red blood').

Original Buddhism was not concerned with legend and primal myths about the origin of humankind and the universe. Siddhartha Gautama, the Buddha or 'enlightened one', was essentially uninterested in the question of the origin of humans, saying 'Inconceivable, O Monks, is this Samsara (the cycle of existence); not to be discovered is any first beginnings of beings.'[3] In addition, Buddhism rejects the belief in a personal creator god claiming that the world goes through successive periods of expansion and contraction, unaffected by the activities of the gods. However, as with the many diverse cultures that Buddhism encountered as it spread from India, it was able to absorb and transform the indigenous religions it encountered.

---

[3] Buddhists and other non-Christians do not use the abbreviations AD and BC. They refer to years under the accepted dating convention as either CE (Common Era) or BCE (Before Common Era).

The racial origins of the Tibetans are complicated. Tibet has absorbed and assimilated a wide range of peoples including the *Ch'iang* (Tibeto-Burmans) the *Yüeh-Chih* (Indo-Europeans) the *T'u yu hun* (Turco-Mongols) the *Hor* (Mongol), the *Dards* and the people from the south called the *Mön* (regarded as aboriginal in some areas). There remains a variety of dialects within this ethnic complexity which achieved a cultural unity because of its tolerant religion. A Tibetan proverb affirms that 'every Lama has his own method of teaching as each valley has its own mode of speech'.

The first signs of Tibet's human occupation were excavated near the town of Chamdo in eastern Tibet where a Neolithic settlement of 4,600 years ago was unearthed. Here, over an area of about 8,000 square metres (2 acres) were found large quantities of stone implements, bone utensils, earthenware and the bones of oxen and sheep. It is thought by some authorities, although not substantiated, that these Neolithic people may have migrated from the Huanghe (Yellow River) valley. Agriculture was established by about 100 BCE[4].

The landscape of Tibet

The indigenous name for Tibet is *P'ö* (pronounced *Bod*), or *P'öyül* and, more romantically, the Land of Snows. Tibet is a vast country perched on the 'roof of the world' at 4,000 metres (13,000 feet) above sea level. The historic map of Tibet, prior to the Chinese invasion in 1949–50, shows the total land area to be 1,100,000 square kilometres (460,000 square miles) – one-eighth the size of the United States and about 5 times the size of Britain. It is traditionally divided into three main provinces of Amdo (North East Tibet), Kham (South East Tibet) and U-Tsang (Central Tibet) although these areas have now been subdivided by the Chinese into smaller administrative areas. The capital is Lhasa (a shortened form of *lha sacha* meaning 'god's place'), an ancient city dating back over 1,300 years whose skyline is still

---

[4] *Digha Niyaka* (3.28ff.)–part of the Discourse Collection of the Theravada Buddhist Canon in which the Buddha argues the Hindu Brahmans.

dominated by the majestic Potala Palace. This once sacred city is now growing at a frightening rate and its built-up area has increased ten times in the past 20 years due to the massive influx of Han Chinese immigrants who now outnumber the native population in their own homeland. The population of Lhasa is 170,000 and Tibet's government in exile estimates the country's total non-Tibetan population to be between 2.5 and 3 million.

Tibet has a unique geography with a landscape that naturally isolates her from her adjacent countries, delineated by the high peaks of the Kunlun and Himalayan mountain ranges. The northern part of Tibet, which covers nearly half the country, is made up largely of a rocky desert plain called Changthang and this intensely arid place has never been able to support towns or settlements of any size. The lower lowland valleys of Southern Tibet, however, contain fertile areas and house the bulk of the nation's population. Here we find the principal cities of Lhasa, Shigatse and Gyantse. The capital city Lhasa is positioned at the focal point of land and water routes and is naturally fortified by mountain ranges.

But no facts or figures can convey the magnificence of the Tibetan landscape with its huge, snow-capped mountains of granite whose blue and purple peaks flow in an endless rhythm over infinite horizons. The landscape seems to perpetually change. A traveller entering another valley or pass sees fantastic, surreal rock shapes or strange melting ice sculptures carved by the hand of nature. At every turn the traveller is greeted by another wealth of colour. Slashes of yellow flowers grip the purple rocks and here and there a few sparse trees cling for life. All is bathed in the running banks of damp cloud that hug the ground and cut through the diaphanous air. On the far horizon, against the brilliant turquoise sky, there may be a hint of green from the few precious areas of grass, the white houses of the country folk or the distant glint of sunlight as it catches the gold roof of a far-off monastery. Tibet is an immortal landscape, vast, void and more glorious than any landscape conceived by the imaginations of artists.

Many people marvel at Tibet's vast silence. In places, waterfalls fall from such huge heights that the traveller has to strain to hear the water hit the rocks in the valley floor so far below. Amongst the majesty and stillness of the mountains the visitor is humbled and perhaps reminded of the Buddhist maxim that all of reality is emptiness. As the modern-day traveller marvels at this landscape so must the first inhabitants have looked in awe upon this mysterious place.

Tibet is a land where one cannot but help be aware of the elements. In the highest zones, the average temperature in the hottest months varies from 4°C to -15°C (39°F to 5°F) and with absolute minimums of around -54°C (-40°F). Snow and hail blizzards are common in the winter, windstorms occur throughout the year and there can be many sudden changes in temperature. Even in summer there can be variations of temperature of 40°C between day and night. It is, then, no surprise that the first inhabitants of Tibet developed a shamanistic religion that worshipped the powers of nature and saw fairies and elemental spirits in every rock, valley and mountain of this strange world. People thought they could recognise the demons of earth, air and water and assumed that these powers had to be assuaged and brought under control by sacrifice, worship and spells.

The dawn of religion

The first Tibetan religion was a form of shamanism that sought to tame these animistic forces. R.A. Stein has called this the 'nameless religion', based upon the worship of the elements and mountain deities. Rituals included the offering of incense to appease the mountain spirits or the setting up of prayer flag 'wind horses' (*lungta*) in prominent passes to attract favour and good auspices. Declarations of truth (*dentsik*) and oaths would be affirmed to the local deities to attract prosperity (*gyangkhug*) and talismans were made and placed in areas where the magical powers were most dominant and where it was considered that the earth was filled with life force (*la-ne*). Talismans were also used in sorcery rites to overpower enemies in a ceremony known as *la-guk*.

Out of this primitive religion evolved the so-called 'religion of humans' (*mi-cho*) which endeavoured to provide an ethical framework for social behaviour. These axioms were communicated by storytellers (*drung*) and singers of riddles (*de'u*) or epic poems. The religion had nine aspects symbolised by the body of a lion. The right foot represented primal myths and stories of the origin of the world and the left foot illustrated stories about the origin of humanity. The hindquarters represented legends about the divisions of the earth of which the right hand symbolised genealogy of the rulers and the left hand symbolised the lineage of the subjects. The neck represents the allegiances of the tribes and the head represents the lines of decent by birth. The tail symbolises songs of bliss.

Bön

The oldest known organised religion of Tibet is called Bön and survives to this day alongside Buddhism. The name Bön refers to 'teaching' or 'religion' and is akin to the Tibetan word *chos* which is similar in meaning to the Sanskrit word *Dharma*, truth, law, teaching. The Tibetans call their land Pö, derived from Bön (Bod). Adherents to Bön are called Bönpos.

Bön is thought to have originated from the religion of Tagzig in Persia which was introduced into the far west of Tibet during the period of the early kings. These Tibetan kings were objects of a divine cult and were thought to be manifestations of sky gods transported from heaven on a sky-chord (*mu*). During this period of history the Bön religion practised animal and, according to Chinese sources, human sacrifice as offerings to the gods of the sky, earth and underworld. The gods of these rituals may have been integrated into Buddhism in later years to become the ferocious, wrathful deities as 'protectors of the faith' that can be seen portrayed in Tibetan art. Buddhism bitterly opposed such blood sacrifices and gradually succeeded in abolishing these rites. However, many traces of the old religious beliefs and symbols still survive, particularly in the sect of Nyingma, 'the old order', which is Tibet's second largest monastic order. Nyingma priests are also not usually required to be celibate. (There is an important relationship between the post-eleventh-century Bönpo and the Nyingma, both schools tracing their origins back to the critical period of the introduction of Buddhism in the eighth century.)

The role of the Bön religion changed with time and the focus of the Bönpo shifted to the execution of funeral rites and rituals for the averting of death through 'ransom' (*lud*). The Bönpo's chief function was connected with the funeral ceremonies of kings and the subsequent cult which took place at the burial mound. This involved complicated ritual which was regulated down to the smallest detail with great stress placed upon the perfect enactment of every part of the procedure.

As Buddhism grew throughout Tibet, the royal patronage shifted away from Bön and the Bönpos soon faced persecution and banishment. There is little documentary evidence about the religion during the period from the eighth to the early eleventh centuries but, during this time, a few dedicated Bönpos such as Drenpa Namkha (ninth century) and Shenchen Luga (tenth century) kept the embers of the religion alight until it was re-established alongside Buddhism.

The religion that was reborn in the eleventh century is, however, different from the original ancient faith and is, in essence, almost Buddhism re-packaged. Despite this, the modern-day Bönpo, and also the Buddhists, consider Bön to be a distinct religion. Whereas Tibetan Buddhists ultimately derive their doctrines from the historical Indian Buddha Shakyamuni[5] they maintain that the true Buddha of our age was Töngpa Shenrab Miwo who lived before Shakyamuni in the mythical land of Olmo Lung Ring, situated at a mysterious location somewhere in the west of Tibet. This mythical land is traditionally described as dominated by Mount Yung-drung Gu-tzeg (meaning edifice of Nine Swastikas), which many identify as Mount Kailash. Swastikas and the number nine are an integral part of the Bön religion but do not have the sinister associations that a European may give to this symbol. The leftward-moving swastika is the sign of the Bön religion whereas the rightward moving swastika is regarded as a Buddhist motif. Stupas and chörtens are

---

[5] Another name for the historical Buddha Siddhartha Gautama meaning 'wise man of the Shakya tribe'. Commonly used by Mahayana Buddhists.

circumnambulated by Buddhists in a clockwise direction whereas the Bönpo travel in an anticlockwise direction.

The Swiss psychologist Carl Jung, founder of Analytical Psychology, points out in his book *Archetypes and the Collective Unconscious* that a 'leftward movement [of the swastika] indicates movement towards the unconscious, while a rightward [clockwise] movement goes towards consciousness. The one is "sinister", the other "right", "rightful", "correct" .... The leftward-spinning eddies spin into the unconscious; the rightward-spinning ones out of the unconscious chaos. The rightward-moving swastika in Tibet is therefore a Buddhist emblem.' From a Jungian standpoint, therefore, the influence of Buddhism upon Bön is for the best.[6]

Tönpa Shenrab Miwo is considered by the Bönpos to be the enlightened teacher of this age and walked this earth in times before the coming of Buddha Shakyamuni. He is held by Bönpos to have propagated Bön throughout the world, including Tibet. Accounts say that 18 enlightened teachers, including the founder Tönpa Shenrab Miwo, will appear in this aeon and to help humankind towards enlightenment.

According to legend, Tönpa Shenrab Miwo first created the Bön creed in heaven. He then vowed at the feet of Shenla Okar, the god of compassion, to guide the people of this world and, at the age of 31, took up a life of austerity in order to spread the teachings and save all beings trapped within the realms of suffering. In time, he arrived in Tibet at the region of Mount Kailash, which is known as the land of Zhang-Zhung and the traditional seat of Bön culture and doctrine.

Bön scriptures are divided into two groups: the *Kanjur*, containing myths, doctrines and biographies of Tönpa Shenrab Miwo, and *Katen*, containing commentarial material, ritual and iconographic texts. Much of the Bön doctrines are virtually identical to those held by Tibetan Buddhism about Buddhahood, the Bodhisattva ideal and so on which I'll explain in Chapter 2.

---

[6]The Bönpo perform ritual act as prescribed by the Bön religion with the same piousness as their Buddhist counterparts and with the ultimate intention of becoming enlightened. Their monks, who are strictly celibate, live according to the highest rules of morality and conduct.

Also, important are the *dzogchen* doctrines held in common with the Nyingmapas which maintain that there is an ineffable state beyond all manifestation and beyond all Buddhas. Westerners mistakenly think only of the Tibetan Buddhist (*chos*) traditions yet do not realise that there is this second great religion in Tibet.

Buddhism enters Tibet

When the first Buddhists crossed the Himalayas they encountered in the early Bön system many beliefs that are completely opposed to the teachings of the Buddha. The original teachings of the Buddha, that you will read about in detail in Chapter 2, offer us a philosophy of life that requires no belief in God, gods or superstition but urges its followers to test the philosophy for themselves by means of meditation. Furthermore, the Buddha teaches that people should not believe what he says just because he says so, but should test out his words and directly experience his teachings. Bön, on the other hand, was closer to a shamanistic religion steeped in ritual, superstition and animism with a separate priesthood that wielded political influence.

The non-violent teachings of Buddhism must have been particularly difficult to expound to a nation of regional tribal warlords under the authority of a divine royal family with ambitions for large-scale conquest. The Bön religion was also sophisticated in that it practised large-scale sacrificial rituals, built intricate tumuli, had court priests and magicians, and worshipped a complex collection of gods governing all aspects family, tribal, regional and national issues.

Yet amazingly, in Tibet the somewhat cerebral philosophy of Buddhism integrated with the instinctive philosophy of Bön. This unusual fusion of opposites, combined with the unique character of the Tibetan people and incubated in one of the world's most magnificent environments, resulted in one of the world's most inspiring sources of wisdom.

But the introduction and spread of Buddhism into Tibet was by no means easy and met with great hostility from the native Bön religion. Not only did it have considerable influence in the court but it was also deeply rooted in the mind and traditions of the commoners. Yet, despite this, Buddhism had its appeal. On the surface it appeared, to the uncouth Tibetans, to be a superior form of magic and on a deeper level it offered the opportunity for anyone to progress spiritually.

It is said in the legends that the Indian king named Rupati, who fled to Tibet after his defeat in the Mahabharata war, was enthroned as their king in 127 BCE by 12 wise Bön priests who believed that he had descended from heaven. They gave him the name Nyatri Tsenpo. But Buddhism is believed to have first entered Tibet from India and China during the second century CE. Tibet's political power expanded under the young warrior king Songtsen Gampo (CE 608–50). He was probably encouraged in his interest by his two wives who were both Buddhists. At this time, Tibet was a powerful warfaring nation and King Gampo posed a sufficient threat to China to be able to demand a Chinese princess as his bride. Emperor Tai Zong, the first of the Tang Dynasty, sent his adopted daughter, Wen Cheng, to Tibet with pomp and ceremony, along with a gold Buddha statue as her dowry. King Gampo also made another alliance by marrying Princess Besa of Nepal and his total of three wives gave birth to the children who founded Tibet's Tubo Dynasty.

Legend has it that the two foreign brides converted Gampo from the Bön faith to Buddhism. They also persuaded him to wear silk instead of sheepskins. In addition, Songtsen Gampo built a fortress on Red Hill (the first Poala) for the brides to live in and he built the Jokhang and Ramoche temples in Lhasa to house the holy Buddha statues.

Songtsen Gampo is said to have sent an intelligent young man, Thonmi Sambhota, to India to collect Buddhist texts and invent a Tibetan system of writing. The new form of writing that Sambhota produced was an incredible intellectual achievement. His orthography was based on that of Kashmir and he adapted its script to the complicated Tibetan language. Within 20 years of its invention, Sambhota's system had come into wide use in Tibet for documents and laws as well as for writing translations of Buddhist texts.

Some authorities claim that King Songtsen Gampo didn't adopt Buddhism at all. He is likely to have been loyal to his ancestral religion which regarded him as a divine being. The enormous burial mound of King Songtsen Gampo, which can still be seen in the Yarlung valley, bears testimony to his faith in which the funeral rites kings included complicated rituals on a large scale with animal and human sacrifice. Despite this, much later when lamas governed Tibet, Songtsen Gampo, the first 'religious king', was proclaimed an incarnation of the Bodhisattva of Compassion and the patron saint of Tibet. His image is often seen in temples wearing a high orange or gold turban with a small Buddha head peeping over the top. His Chinese wife, Wen Cheng, is always on the viewer's right with his Nepalese wife, Besa, on the viewer's left.

The teacher Padmasambhava

The next four generations of kings after Songtsen Gampo dedicated themselves to wars of conquest and, during these times, Tibet became a powerful and much feared nation. Buddhism continued to gain a more sure foothold by absorbing many of the features of the old Bön faith which, in particular, corresponds with the beliefs of Tantrism.

The second great king of the Tubo Dynasty was Trisong Deutsen (755–97) who, like Gampo, was an accomplished warlord. His fearsome armies campaigned from Samarkand to as far afield as Chang'an, the capital of China. Trisong Deutsen is known as Tibet's second 'religious king' and under his rule Buddhism became firmly established in Tibet.

Trisong Deutsen also encouraged famous Buddhist teachers from India and China, two in particular were a Mahayana scholar called Shantarakshita and a Tantric master called Padmasambhava. During this period the task of translating Buddha's teachings was carried out with great enthusiasm. It is believed that 108 Indian scholars were employed in this mammoth work of translation. In the era that followed, thousands of temples were constructed and a decree was issued by King Trisong Deutsen that every monk should be supported by seven households. He founded Samyey, Tibet's first monastery, in 779 where Tibetans could be trained as monks.

Padmasambhava's efforts were particularly influential. He spent his days travelling the country explaining to the most promising disciples the most advanced Tantric teachings and encouraged them on long retreats. Legends claim that he wrestled with and tamed the tribal gods and elemental spirits and eventually converted them to Buddhism. Thus, Tibet's gods of the rivers, mountains, sky, earth and sacred spring now followed the Dharma and, most importantly, could be considered as part of the Tibetan Buddhist religion. What this probably indicates is that Padmasambhava's Tantric form of Buddhism with its leaning towards magical practices could more easily blend with the Bön beliefs of the local people, and appealed to them more than the intellectualism of Buddhism.

Padmasambhava, better known as Guru Rimpoche in Tibet, is considered to be one of Tibet's greatest saints. He was considered to have had a miraculous birth, not born by woman but found inside a lotus flower. Padmasambhava was believed to possess magical powers and is the original author of the great and important treatise *The Tibetan Book of the Dead* that describes the spiritual planes that exist after death and gives instructions to find liberation or a suitable womb for rebirth.

During King Trisong Deutsen's reign Buddhism had grown in Tibet and the monks began to have more and more political influence. Fifty years after Detsen's death the power of the monks reached a climax when his grandson turned over his whole administration to a monk. But this pious king was assassinated and his brother, Lang Darma, seized the throne.

Tibetan Buddhism's dark age

Comparatively soon after these golden years of Buddhist flowering, known as the era of Tibet's Religious Kings, the Buddhist expansion came to an end. Lang Darma who reigned from 836–42 set about extinguishing Buddhism and returning the nation to the religion of Bön. A period of confusion ensued when King Lang Darma persecuted Buddhists. The monasteries were closed down, scriptures destroyed and the monks were made to disrobe, sent into exile or forced to join the army. Practising Buddhism was made a capital offence and Tibet entered a dark age. Without the guidance of the priestly class, Tibet collapsed into enclaves ruled by rival clans.

However, during these difficult times some monks went underground and continued the Buddha's teachings in secret. King Lang Darma succeeded in suppressing the voice of Buddhism but could not extinguish its spirit. In particular, Mar Shakya Yeshi, Yogejung and Tsang Rabsel, who were holders of the monastic lineage of the Abbot Shantarakshita, escaped to the north-eastern (Domey) region of Tibet to revive the flame of faith. Here they were helped by two Chinese monks (*ho Shang*) and gave full ordination to Lachen Gongpa Rabsel. This is considered to be the start of the revival of the Tibetan monastic community. Likewise in western Tibet (Ngari) the teachings of Buddhism were expanded by Sadhupala and the great Kashmiri scholar Shakyashri; the monastic lineages were multiplied and the Buddhist community grew. From these sanctuaries ordained Buddhist monks returned to central Tibet, Buddhism was revived and a building programme was begun to re-establish the temples and monasteries.

Gradually, peace returned and the embers of Buddhism began to rekindle a flame.

The great teacher Atisha

Buddhism went through its renaissance in western Tibet during the reign of King Lha Lama Yeshe Ö who, like the religious kings from long ago, sent intelligent young Tibetans to the thriving Buddhist community at Kashmir. Historians call this the 'second introduction' of Buddhism into Tibet which was epitomised in the life work of two great men. The first was a Tibetan named Rinchen Zangpo (958–1055) who studied in Kashmir and returned full of wisdom and loaded with manuscripts that he translated. The second was an Indian master from Bengal named Atisha Dipamkara Shrijnana (982–1054) who the king invited to Tibet.

Atisha is an immensely important figure in the history of Tibetan Buddhism and is known as *Jowo Jey,* meaning 'spiritual master who is himself a Buddha'. Atisha's teachings dispelled many misunderstandings about Buddhist doctrine then current and he revived the teachings that, to this day, sit at the heart of Tibetan Buddhism. In particular, he composed the famous text *A Lamp on the Path of Enlightenment* which established the format for the Lamrim texts found in the Tibetan Buddhist tradition. His teachings also were influenced by Tantric scriptures of Vajrayana Buddhism with its parallel movements in Hinduism.

The Tibetans welcomed this well-spoken and educated 60-year-old Atisha as a Buddha in human form. He had a superhuman status, a perfect and enlightened being like the Buddha Shakyamuni (Gautama). His stay in Tibet lasted only 12 years yet during this time he established a synthesis of all the key methods of Buddhism for developing people. His teachings embodied an integration of methods that communicated the Buddhist wisdom to the lower classes and the uneducated. Atisha's influence transformed the violent, warrior mentality of the ordinary Tibetan into a peaceful nation of spiritual seekers. In addition, he clarified the Tantric Scriptures that could so easily be misinterpreted by the simple peasants. (Some of these texts contain symbolic references to cannibalism, murder and sexual excess.) Instead, Atisha and his successors presented a system of teachings that addressed the perennial problems of taming the mind, living in a monastery, overcoming materialism, cultivating compassion and attaining the wisdom of the realisation of selflessness.

Atisha also had an almost encyclopaedic knowledge of Buddhist literature and Tantra. He stressed the fact that the truth of Buddhism lay not only in the authoritative canonical texts but could be taught directly by the spiritual mentor. This mentor, master, lama or guru is the key element in understanding and putting into practice the true teachings. In this way, Atisha showed that the original Buddha's teachings had to be adapted to the individual and the society in which they were being applied. They were not isolated abstract truths but part of real life. The mentor's job is to show how the teachings specifically apply to each practitioner.

This focus on the spiritual mentor, usually called Lamaism, is one of the attributes that distinguishes Tibetan Buddhism from other forms of Buddhism around the world. (In the word 'lama', the syllable 'la' means transcendent wisdom; 'ma' denotes motherly love and compassion. These two parts are united in Ultimate Awareness.) However, some Buddhists believe that Tibetan Buddhism has thereby lost the original teaching of the Buddha Shakyamuni. But Tibetans would argue that Lamaism not only teaches how to apply the teachings but has allowed Buddhism to evolve over the centuries and given it the ability to adapt to the needs of the individual and modern society. It furthermore presupposes that there have been many enlightened teachers before and since Shakyamuni and that there will be more to come. This attitude leaves the door open for Buddhism to grow and progress continually.

Atisha and his many disciples, which included Drom Tönpa who founded the Kadampa tradition, had a far-reaching influence upon Tibetan society that resulted in a mushrooming of Buddhism in Tibet from the eleventh to the fourteenth century. A religious fervour swept the country and the monastic way of life became firmly established throughout the whole society. Also during this period Tibet's contact with the Indian traditions was restored and the influence of different masters and teachers resulted in many distinctly different teaching lineages. Over a period of time there arose four great schools of Tibetan Buddhism: Sakya, Kagyu, Gelug and Nyingma. We will look at these in detail later but first we will look at Milarepa, Tibet's greatest black magician turned saint and poet.

The great teacher Milarepa

In 1042, just two years before Atisha began his missionary work in Western and Central Tibet, the greatest and most revered of Tibetan Buddhist masters was born. Milarepa was a disciple of Marpa (1012–99) who came from a family of rich merchants in the Lhodrag region of Southern Tibet. Marpa was a highly respected teacher who began his studies with the translator Drogmi and who journeyed to Nepal and India in search of spiritual teachers. The most important of these was the scholar

Naropa, a great adept of Tantra. Marpa's teachings were essentially the same as those brought back from India by Atisha and Drogmi and encouraged the monastic way of life, the practice of renunciation, transcendence, wisdom of voidness, compassion and Tantric Yoga.

Milarepa was Marpa's most important disciple. Like Marpa, he came from a wealthy family but he was disinherited by his wicked uncle when his father died. Milarepa's paternal uncle and aunt made a promise to his dying father to act as trustees to the estate until the seven-year-old Milarepa reached his maturity. As soon as Milarepa's father died, the uncle and aunt seized the estate and denied ever having promised to be the trustees. Milarepa was treated with the grossest cruelty and injustice by his greedy and selfish uncle and aunt. He and his mother now faced a life of abject poverty and misery.

It was Milarepa's mother who first turned to black magic in order to seek vengeance against these wrong doers. She saw in the youthful and devoted Milarepa a ready instrument to fulfil her scheme. She possessed a small plot of land in her own name which she sold to pay for a special education in sorcery for her son. Single-mindedly Milarepa strove towards the destruction of his evil relatives. He consulted the Bön lamas, who were masters of the black arts, and with their guidance evoked secret magic to wreak his revenge. At a wedding feast for the uncle's eldest son, Milarepa unleashed his powers to bring down the home of the uncle and aunt, killing them and most of the wedding guests. When the villagers discovered that Milarepa was behind the events that had happened, they sought him out in order to exact their own vengeance.

Milarepa's mother heard of the villagers' plan and warned him. She advised him to cause fierce hailstorms to destroy all their crops and, using the black arts, Milarepa cast a spell. A fierce hailstorm raged and ruined the uncle's estate. Admitting defeat, the uncle returned the patrimony.

But the moral consequences of his crimes consumed Milarepa. His mind whirled with remorse and he came close to committing suicide. He considered the karmic consequences of his moral decline and decided he would reform. With the same impeccable determination that drove his quest for the secrets of black magic, Milarepa renounced worldly goods and now began the search for a teacher who could give him the keys to enlightenment and liberation.

Milarepa experienced a feeling of a deeper order in life, a call to explore the meaning of existence. His is the quest of sinner turned saint. The heroic story has universal appeal and we see a man develop from avenging black magician to powerful yogi. His struggle shows the way to spiritual freedom and complete self-realisation.

Milarepa's transformation and realisation of the Dharma takes place at the feet of the great lama and translator Marpa who he met at Marpa's country home. At first Marpa refuses to take him in, as Milarepa could not pay, so Milarepa offers his own person, body and soul, so entering a long and cruel apprenticeship.

The fierce Marpa forced Milarepa to go through many terrible ordeals in order to overcome the negative karma that he had created by killing so many people. He was convinced Milarepa's karma was so bad that the desired transformation could not be achieved by normal training. Consequently, Milarepa was required to fulfil a series of dispiriting and brutally demanding tasks which included endlessly building and tearing down a tower. Only after Milarepa was brought to the brink of despair and suicide did Marpa grant him the secrets of the teaching. Satisfied at last, Marpa taught Milarepa, initiated him and sent him to a life of contemplation, rather than scholarship like his other disciples. Marpa's objective had been to ensure that Milarepa's motives were absolutely pure—knowledge and liberation must be sought for the benefit of all sentient beings and not just for one's own personal enlightenment.

After his training with Marpa, Milarepa lived a life of asceticism and retreat which was in direct contrast to the external life of Marpa. He learned to live in the Himalayan winter wearing only a white cotton robe. He practised the advanced magical yogas and, in particular, mastered the generation of heat through the power of meditation. It is said that he ate nothing but nettles until his hair turned green and developed great occult powers and clairvoyance, which he used, say the legends, in contests of magic to convince the Bön priest of Buddhism's superiority.

In time, Milarepa became even greater than his teacher and within 12 years had become a perfectly enlightened Adept. He travelled all over Tibet and taught thousands of people. He is perhaps most famous for his musical accomplishments and taught his most profound philosophy in song and verse. His thousands of exuberant songs express his enlightened vision and celebrated the joys of solitude and of the natural world. They became immensely popular and are still sung today. Although Milarepa suffered much in order to attain enlightenment, many of his own pupils achieved the glimpse of illumination spontaneously on hearing his songs.

The story of Milarepa illustrates how an ordinary man can become a perfect Buddha. He thus became an example for millions of Tibetans who have sought their own salvation. The songs and poems of Milarepa are beloved by all and his life symbolises the Buddhist maxim that anyone, even a sinner, can attain enlightenment in a single lifetime. In some ways, his life resembled that of St Francis of Assisi– a sinner in youth who repented and who devoted his later years to selfless works and ended his life as a saint.

Milarepa lived to the age of 83, a wise, inspired, compassionate and, perhaps a little eccentric, teacher who captured the hearts of all Tibetans. Tibetan art portrays him smiling ecstatically, with his hand raised to his ear as he sings.

Marpa ('the translator') and Milarepa ('the cotton clad') were never ordained as monks and represent a type of Buddhist Tantric yogin very different from the monastic ideals propagated by Atisha. They introduced a new type of religious system that was highly personal, introduced poetry and embraced the individual's own spontaneous feelings and observations. It is a tradition that continues to the present day.

According to Milarepa, this teacher–pupil relationship can extend beyond the human. He explains that there are three types of lamas: the 'external lama' who instructs on the physical level; the 'inner lama' which is one's own power of understanding the teaching; the 'inmost lama' which is one's own inmost awareness. Marpa was the external lama but Milarepa was to spiritually progress to the point where he realised the 'inmost lama' within himself.

Since the times of Marpa and Milarepa, different schools of Tibetan Buddhism have evolved and, superficially, it appears that there are many divisions within Tibetan Buddhism. Over the centuries, history has seen many heated debates between the orders over points of doctrine and its interpretation. But the differences are only in the detail. In essence, all the major schools of Tibetan Buddhism believe in the same basic precepts. They all consider Shakyamuni to be the main Buddha of this world-epoch and believe that a Buddha is a being who has transcended the human to become superhuman. They also all agree that there have been many other Buddhas since Shakyamuni who have lived in Tibet and are responsible for Tibetan civilisation.

It is also universally accepted that human life is a unique opportunity to progress towards enlightenment and that many ordinary Tibetans have become Buddhas. This goal brings freedom from suffering, inner peace, liberation and the highest form of happiness. To help others, many enlightened beings have reincarnated over many lives and continue to teach their disciples who, in turn, will also become Buddhas. In this way the lotus of enlightenment expands to embrace all life. All schools strive towards this same transcendent wisdom. Their differences of doctrine lie only in the methods that can be used for attaining Buddhahood.

Chapter 2
Tibetan Buddhism

The life of Siddhartha Gautama

Siddhartha Gautama was born into a prosperous aristocratic family of the Shakya clan (Kshatriya class) of Nepal and northern India some time around 560 BCE. Legend has it that his father was king of the Shakyas and Siddhartha himself a prince: 'A King Suddhodhana by name was my father. A Queen Maya by name was the mother that bore me. The Royal capital was the city of Kapilavatthu.' (*Digha Nikaya 14*) The legends and writings also say that, like the virgin birth of Christ hundreds of years later, the baby Siddhartha's conception occurred miraculously through the soul descending directly from heaven into his mother Maya's womb. There is no mention of a father involved and some sources stress that the Queen conceived while undertaking a temporary vow of chastity.

The Tibetan Buddhists claim that the Buddha-to-be deliberately chose his mother's womb. He saw that King Suddhodhana was of pure lineage and that the families of both the king and queen were flawless for seven generations. In addition, his mother Maya had already vowed to give birth to Buddhas many lives previously. Before the assembled gods in the heavenly worlds he crowned Maitreya (the Buddha to come) as his successor and entered his mother's womb in order to manifest supreme Buddhahood on earth.

Maya felt a great light enter her body and her womb. The Tibetan version of the story now becomes more mythical than factual. The story says that the womb now becomes a vast space and within it are pagodas within pagodas made of serpentine sandalwood. The spirit of the Buddha-to-be (also called Bodhisattva Shvetaketu) enters the womb from the right side and appears as a young snow-white elephant with six tusks. He then transforms into a six-month-old child, wearing a robe and seated cross legged on a throne. From the throne within the womb he converses with the gods, dragons, giants etc, and develops and liberates countless disciples. The story becomes even more complex and we are told how, for example, 500 young white elephants come down and touch his feet.

Maya's pregnancy must have been an extremely uncomfortable experience. The baby was born from the right side of his mother's body and it is said there were many miraculous happenings such as foals, baby elephants and calves born by the thousands. The parents chose the name Siddhartha meaning 'Accomplisher of Aims'. Just like in the nativity story of Christianity, they were visited by some wise men. The Himalayan sage called Asita and his clairvoyant could see the gods rejoicing and saying how a perfect Buddha had been born into the world and they called to pay homage to the Bodhisattva. To the horror of the father, he prophesied that the boy would grow up to be one of two things: a great king or a Buddha. If he saw the suffering of the world his destiny would be the latter.

His mother Maya is said to have passed away seven days after the birth and to have been reborn in heaven. Siddhartha was cared by for by Mahapajapati Gotami, his mother's sister who also married his father.

The first full-length biography of the life of the Buddha was not written down until the first century CE by the poet Ashvaghosa and it is not surprising to find that after 500 years legendary and mythological details have found their way into the original story. And the imaginative Tibetans may have exaggerated the story further. The earlier source is the scriptures of the Pali Canon of the Theravadins which relates many events from the Buddha's life but not in chronological order. Although this was supposedly collected together about three months after the Buddha's death, it was not actually written down until the first century BCE.

According to the Pali Canon scriptures, the Bodhisattva[1] lived an opulent life of luxury, with exquisite food, gorgeous clothing and many servants. But he was not happy. He felt a deep sense of dissatisfaction and a desire to find deeper meaning. The same spiritual malady affects our own modern society and the Buddha's yearning for spirituality strikes a chord with many people today. Most of us have a standard of living comparable with the kings and queens of old yet our opulence, greed and materialism seem never to satisfy. Many people feel spiritually hollow. We indulge ourselves in pleasures, amusements and distractions on a scale never seen before throughout history, yet spiritually we are beggars.

According to the legends, Siddhartha was married at 16 to a neighbouring princess whose name is usually given as Yasodhara and whose hand he won in a contest of warrior skills. The commentaries and legends say that the prince led a sheltered life and was deliberately kept away from all experience of sickness, old age or death in an attempt by his father to prevent him fulfiling the prophesies and renouncing the world.

Siddhartha has everything he could wish for: a beautiful wife, riches, health. Yet his heart still feels the pull towards realisation. At the age of 29 Siddhartha's yearning for spiritual knowledge reached a head. Whilst on an excursion from the palaces with his charioteer Channa, he saw four sights that changed his life: a tired, wrinkled old man; a man in terrible pain from illness; a corpse in a funeral procession; a religious ascetic. Thus it dawns on the Bodhisattva that the world is filled with suffering and that all things, including himself, are subject to ageing, disease and death. The sight of the ascetic triggers his decision to renounce the transient pleasure of life and seek a solution to these problems in self-denial.

[1] Means 'being of enlightenment' and can refer to (a) a being who dedicates himself or herself to obtaining enlightenment not for themselves but in order to help others; (b) Shakyamuni Buddha in his life/lives previous to enlightenment.

The Tibetan accounts describe how he went to the roof of his palace and vowed to attain enlightenment quickly for the sake of all beings. The sky filled with deities, gods, fairies and dragons all carrying various offerings. The palaces guards were overcome and a divine ladder transported him to his horse Kanthaka. Led by the ancient gods of India and with his tearful charioteer, Chandra, beside him he covered hundreds of miles and saw the spot where three past Buddhas had cut their hair in renunciation of the world. Siddhartha commanded Chandra to take his ornaments and horse Kanthaka back to the palace. Then he slowly cut his long, oiled, black hair and threw it triumphantly into the sky where, says the legends, it was borne aloft by the god Indra. Instead of his fine silk robes the Bodhistattva now donned the simple orange robe of a monk, his only other possession being a begging bowl.

His noble steed, Kanthaka, returned to the palace riderless and in sorrow expired while his master crossed the Ganga and entered the kingdom of Magadha in search of his longed-for enlightenment.

'The Great Renunciation', as it is called, took place on the same night as his wife Yasodhara bore him a son, Rahula. In some accounts it is said that Siddhartha left home secretly at the dead of night and crept into his wife's bedroom to glimpse his newborn son. He deliberately avoided waking his wife or looking at the baby's face in case it weakened his resolve. Some have said that to seek enlightenment is the highest form of selfishness and will quote this part of the story to illustrate their point. To the Buddhist enlightenment is sought, not for personal liberation, but for the benefit of all sentient beings. Siddhartha's actions are symbolic of the complete detachment necessary in order to achieve this goal.

The Bodhistattva was not alone in his quest. Indian society, during this period of its history, was deeply interested in the fundamental questions of existence. Competing meditation teacher and philosophical schools were everywhere and religious debate was a popular pastime. Common practices were extreme asceticism and various meditation and yogic techniques. It was generally accepted that such practices could free one's soul from the limitation of the corporal body into eternal peace. These were spiritually exciting times.

In this spiritually charged land, Siddhartha spend six years wandering and learning from the most famous teachers of northern India. Two were of particular importance: Kalama and Uddaka Ramaputta who taught the Bodhisattva how to achieve advanced levels of mediation known in Buddhism as the mental state of 'nothingness' and 'neither perception-nor-nonperception'. His search finally led him to join five young Brahmins on the banks of the river Nairanjana who had undertaken a life of extreme austerity. The Bodhisattva embraced the way of life completely and is said to have made four times the effort of the others. Accounts say that he lived on one grain of rice a day and sat cross-legged in *Samadhi* (mental discipline) for six years. He wouldn't wash, wore horsehair clothes and pulled out his hair and beard. Many people of the time, such as the Jains, believed that harsh treatment of the body would lead to liberation and these traditions continue in India to this day. Some still seek out dreadful places to live such as cremation grounds, infested forests or beds of thorns. They may eat nothing or feast on funeral ash or human excrement.

But after six years of this gruelling ordeal, undertaken at the prime of life, Siddhartha decided that he was on a false path. He had to find the middle way between the extremes that he had known in life. To the disgust of his mendicant comrades, he quit the ascetic ordeals, breathed freely and began to eat ordinary food. He washed in the Nairanjana river and put on clean clothes. Two maidens gave him milk. Tibetan accounts say that it was served from a golden urn and contained the essence of a thousand cows. Certainly, after six years of fasting it must have tasted good. The story continues to say that on drinking the milk the Bodhisattva was restored to his former health, displayed the 32 major marks and 80 minor signs of enlightenment and was surrounded by a halo of light and spiritual beings.

Siddhartha had learnt tremendous self-control and had overcome fear, desire and disgust. Now, with the same unrelenting energy and determination, he decided to concentrate on meditation instead.

The enlightenment of Shakyamuni Buddha

Although it may appear as a defeat to turn away from the path of self-mortification, it was actually a great victory for Siddhartha. He had overcome the human tendency to refuse to admit that one has made a mistake and been proved wrong. Siddhartha had renounced everything to follow this path yet he was prepared to challenge his course in the desire to find truth. He did not mind losing his disciples, he did not mind being on his own again; instead, he admitted he had made a mistake and continued his quest.

Eventually, after five premonitory dreams and on the same night as accepting the meal, Siddhartha sat under a tree in Bodhgaya and spent the whole night in meditation. He vowed to himself to make one last effort and that he would not move form the spot until he had fulfiled his quest for enlightenment. Tibetan art depicts this moment with the Buddha-to-be sitting on a heap of *kusa* grass beneath the spreading branches of the *ficus religious* or sacred fig that was later to be known as the Bodhi tree, or 'tree of enlightenment'.[2] Surrounding him on all sides are thousands of fearsome fire-breathing demons and deformed figures. Some shoot arrows, wield spears or tear up mountains. The myth relates that the Shakyamuni Buddha was confronted by Mara (the Buddhist personification of change and death, often called 'the evil one') and his army of evil forces. Mara[3] tempts the Buddha in the hope that he will give up his quest.

This is a symbol of the difficulties every individual will encounter on the struggle towards enlightenment. The temptations represent our fears, doubts and the desire to return to worldly pursuits and pleasures. But the Buddha took no notice of this display and, seeing all things as like magic illusions, had no

---

[2] The Bodhi tree reminds us of the 'tree of knowledge' from the Book of Genesis in the Bible of which human beings were forbidden to eat. The holy tree is an archetypal symbol that links heaven and earth. Just as the tree can reach high in the sky only because it is strongly rooted in the earth so the full development of consciousness requires the assistance of the unconscious.

[3] Also known as 'The Trickster', Mara rules over the worlds belonging to *kamaloka*, or the 'realm of sensuous desire' which includes our own human world. But also, as a symbol of death Mara rules over the entire universe.

fear of these devil armies. The Bodhisattva had gained enough merit and self-control to conquer these temptations. As the various arrows and missiles touched his aura they turned into flowers and fell to the ground. Buddha continued meditating. Mara then changed his tactics and tried to seduce the Buddha. He summoned his three daughters and ordered them to dance in the most seductive manner. Again, the Buddha remained in serene meditation; nothing could persuade him from this path. Finally, Mara accepted defeat and together with his confused daughters withdrew, leaving the Buddha alone beneath the Bodhi tree.

Many texts elaborate this story and tell of how Mara tried to entice Buddha to take up his princely duties; how Buddha ate up the devil armies and frightened them with a flaming sword and we read tales of how he touched the earth and called the earth goddess Prithvivi as his witness to the truth. The Tibetan *Yamantaka Tantra* says he conquered the devil by arising in the bodies of the red-and-black Yamantakas and in other Tibetan texts are told stories of how he left his body by the river bank and in his astral body entered Akanishta heaven where he merged with the great mandala of the diamond realm. Of course, these stories are mythical ways to describe what happened. The truth is that the Buddha sat alone beneath the Bodhi tree and no man witnessed what really happened. These stories, like the story of the temptation of Christ on the mountain top, are symbols that represent the stages of enlightenment and the obstacles that everyone will one day have to overcome for themselves.

After 49 days of intensive meditation Siddhartha attained final enlightenment as a result of which the prince-turned-ascetic became the Buddha. Shakyamuni Buddha's realisation of the ultimate truth of reality unfolded in stages like a lotus unfurling its petals. The first stage is a kind of detached and calm thinking, where one feels joy and peace but is only just removed form everyday consciousness. In the next stage, Shakyamuni Buddha became detached from the chatter of the mind and transcended thought to enter a state of exalted rapture. In the third stage, he reached an even purer joy until he enters the fourth and final level of consciousness. Here even joy fades away leaving a mind so peaceful and clear that it can perceive directly into reality.

These four stages of consciousness prepared Shakyamuni Buddha to realise the superconscious states. The first of these realisations occurred in the first watch of the night (6 p.m. to 10 p.m) when he spontaneously remembered all of his past existence. He recalled tens of thousands of lives in detail as if living them again in their entirety. Everyone has these detailed memories locked away somewhere inside them. I've seen ordinary people describe their other lives in detail under hypnosis. Sometimes they have given facts that we verified in the public records. Also, when I knelt at the feet of my own guru, Sai Baba, in India I saw my past lives flash before me like a video on fast forward. The truth is that everyone can attain the exalted states that Shakyamuni Buddha and others after him have revealed to us. Some Buddhists claim that some of his previous lives are retold in the Jataka tales of the Pali Canon. Shakyamuni is the Buddha of this age, Kali Yuga, before him lived Buddha Dipankara, and the Enlightened One of the next age will be Buddha Maitreya. Someone who has attained enlightenment departs from the wheel of life and no longer needs to be reborn. However, Buddha Shakyamuni resolved to remain in the stream of life in order that he may teach people the truth as Dipankara once had and as Maitreya will in centuries to come.

Shakyamuni Buddha was filled with compassion when he saw how all other beings are bound to this process of life after life in a seemingly pointless cycle. As the night progressed at the next watch (10 p.m. to 2 a.m.) he gained another superconscious insight, known in Buddhism as 'the heavenly eye'. His awareness expanded so that he had direct vision of all the possible dimensions and realms of existence. He saw not only the human realms with people moving between earthly, heavenly and hell states but saw the realms of the gods, ghosts, elementals, fairies and the multitude of animals kingdoms. In all of these 'many mansions' he observed that all beings made their own suffering through their own behaviour. A Christian may see similarities again in the teachings of Christ: 'As ye sow, so shall ye reap.'

In Buddhism this law of cause and effect is called *karma*. The equilibrating law of karma is also expounded in the Hindu scriptures. In the course of natural law, each man by his thoughts and actions becomes the moulder of his destiny. Whatever actions he has set in motion must return to him as their starting point like a circle of events. It is the ultimate justice and man's karma follows him from incarnation to incarnation until fulfiled or spiritually transcended. Shakyamuni Buddha saw these eternal laws unfolding and felt pity for all beings who endlessly went through this cyclic process without knowing why or how to escape it.

At the third watch (2 a.m. to 6 a.m.) Shakyamuni Buddha attained absolute knowledge and absolute enlightenment. For him, karma had lost its object, since it is the same as Dharma, the law of the Absolute. The enlightenment that he realised is impossible to put into words because it is beyond words, form or even thought itself. It can be known but never, even by Shakyamuni Buddha, expressed in its entirety. It consists of a perfect peace, bliss and the unshakeable knowledge that you have experienced absolute Truth. It is infinite joy, infinite bliss and infinite compassion.

This breakthrough of realisation coincided with the rising of the sun at 6 a.m. Siddhartha had defeated the forces of Mara, had seen through the illusionary ego and extinguished all mental defilement. The struggle was now over; he has realised the everlasting, supreme, bliss and, like the sun he saw rising in the morning sky, had awoken from the dark night of the soul. He had not just glimpsed Truth but had become one with it. He was now the Buddha.

Enlightenment is best described as a state of being rather than as an insight into reality. From the point of view of wisdom it is the direct insight into the nature of reality and into truth. This is not an intellectual knowledge but a direct merging with this truth. With it comes the release from ignorance, worries, sorrow and all unhappiness. And, as a bonus perhaps, we experience the ecstatic bliss of pure being. This state is a real possibility for everyone who has taken human birth. Known as 'the heart's release', Buddhists of all creeds seek this same goal. The Buddhist name for this indescribable state, beyond existence and non-existence, where all craving, ignorance and suffering are eliminated is *Nirvana*. It can be achieved both in this life and after death.

The word 'Nirvana' literally means 'blown out', symbolising that the fires of greed, hatred and ignorance are existinguished. Nirvana is first of all cessation, it is the ending of the cycle of life (*samsara*) and the final release from suffering. This concept is quite difficult for Westerners to grasp and at first glance may appear like total annihilation of everything we hold dear. It seems to say that by destroying ourselves we escape suffering. The soul commits suicide in the penultimate selfish act.

But what Shakyamuni Buddha is describing is reminiscent of the same mystical experience that men have described at other times and in other cultures. For example, the Greek neoplatonist philosopher Plotinus experienced a fusion of this soul with God. He taught that everything is wholeness, everything is one. Many other Western philosophers have argued that what we call 'I' is not the true 'I' and, at times, it is possible to have short glimpses of greater 'I'. Some mystics call it God or the 'cosmic spirit', the infinite, nature or the universe. Similar ideas to those expressed by Shakyamuni Buddha can be found in the philosophies of Déscartes, Spinoza, Locke, Bjerkley, Kant and Kierkegaard. In particular, Schopenhauer's (1788–1860) great achievement lay in his recognising the intrinsic dignity of human consciousness which he saw standing above all gods, and as the source of all things – a truth he rediscovered independently. Also, the Christian mystic Angelus Silensius (1624–77) likened this merging with the infinite to a droplet becoming one with the ocean: 'Every drop becomes the sea when it flows oceanward, just as the last soul ascends and thus becomes the Lord.'

Edwin Arnold's epic poem *The Light of Asia*, which aims to present the life of the Buddha as understood by a Theravadin, or Southern Buddhist, describes the enlightenment is a similar way:

> *The Dew is on the lotus! – rise, Great Sun!*
> *And lift my leaf and mix me with the wave.*
> Om mani padme hum, *the Sunrise comes!*
> *The Dewdrop slips into the shining sea!*

These ideas that are at the heart of Eastern mysticism and Buddhism can be hard for many Westerners to grasp. In Judaism, Christianity and Islam the mystic emphasises that this union is with a personal God. Although God is present in the world, nature and the human soul he also transcends the world. However, in Eastern religions it is usual to emphasise that the mystic experience is a total fusion with God. Buddhism does not believe in an independent creator God yet, as you can see, the Truth that Shakyamuni Buddha reveals to us is, at its essence, the same as what it at the heart of most philosophies and religions,

Enlightenment communicated

For several weeks after his enlightenment, Shakyamuni Buddha continued to meditate near the River Niranjana in order to assimilate his experience. Initially, he believed that what had happened to him was impossible to communicate to others. However, he quickly realised that the very nature of his awakening impelled him to share his experience in a spirit of compassion.

During this seven-day period, Shakyamuni Buddha had a vision that expresses the nature of enlightenment and humanity's struggle towards consciousness. He saw it as a lake of lotus plants where some were open, some in bud and others tightly shut and still buried in the mud. Men and women were like this. Some had fully opened to the light whereas others were still emerging from the mud of ignorance. Inspired by his insight, he recognised that a few people might already be at a stage where they were open enough to receive his teachings. It was his duty to share his new-found insight with others.

Shakyamuni Buddha first thought of his old meditation teachers who he considered had come closest to the truth but he soon discovered that they were dead. His thoughts then turned to his five ascetic companions who had shared with him the strenuous ordeals of self-denial for so many years. He set out to the Deer Park 160 kilometres (100 miles) away in Benares where they were living.

At first, the five ascetics refused to listen to him or even greet him but gradually they were impressed by his demeanour and the overwhelming power of his words. Soon they understood that they were in the presence of a person who had directly perceived the truth. To them Shakyamuni Buddha preached his first sermon, which is known as the Deer Park Sermon, or the 'Setting in Motion of the Wheel of the Law'.

His preaching was so powerful that one of the ascetics on hearing that 'all that is arising is subject to cessation' achieved immediate, spontaneous enlightenment and formally committed himself to following the Shakyamuni Buddha and his teachings. Following another sermon on the nature of the self, the other four followed suit.

And so began Shakyamuni Buddha's ministry. For the next 45 years he spent nine months of every year roaming the vast tract of North East India propagating his teaching and enlightening others. He spoke to men and women from every caste and creed and soon people flocked in their hundreds to be in his awe-inspiring presence. Buddhism spread like wildfire. By the time of Shakyamuni Buddha's death at the age of 88 his teachings had spread to 7 nations covering an area of 130,000 square kilometres (50,000 square miles). During his lifetime he enabled hundreds, perhaps thousands, of other people to gain the enlightenment that he had realised

The basic teachings of Shakyamuni Buddha

The teachings of Shakyamuni Buddha are known as the Dharma a word which also means truth, law, order, duty and righteousness. The exact detail of Shakyamuni Buddha's message to humankind is, to this day, surrounded by controversy and within the vast scriptures are many contradictions. The Tibetan Buddhist believes that these initial teachings of Shakyamuni Buddha are only the preliminary teachings of an endless unfoldment of knowledge. Each person can approach this same truth in their own way and within their own cultural background. But most importantly, we must remember that Shakyamuni Buddha taught us that we should not believe just because he said so, but should experience enlightenment for ourselves. To understand the Dharma we must think things out, and see it in our meditation and daily lives. On his deathbed, as Shakyamuni Buddha lay dying from food poisoning at Kusinara, he criticised his distressed devotee Ananda for being upset. Had he not listened to his teachings? All things are impermanent and the Dharma should now be their teacher. His last words prompted his followers to be the masters of their destiny saying: 'Subject to decay are all compounded things, so be mindful and vigilant in working out your own salvation.' Shakyamuni Buddha then entered a state of deep meditation and in total peace and calm, merged forever into Nirvana.[4]

At the Deer Park, Shakyamuni Buddha preached a sermon that is the best known and most important statement of Buddhist teaching. He explained that he had discovered Four Noble Truths that are the key to understanding the nature of ourselves and existence.

The First Noble Truth – The Existence of Suffering (Dukkha)

Shakyamuni Buddha explained that everything we know is suffering: birth, ageing, sickness, death, sorrow, pain, grief, associating with what is loathed, separation from what is loved and not getting what one wants. By suffering, Shakyamuni Buddha used the ancient Indian word *dukkha* which can mean anything from actual physical pain to a sense of hollowness and dissatisfaction. It is a word difficult to translate into Western language and is perhaps best described as 'unsatifactoriness'.

Today, we are all made aware by the media of worldwide poverty, famine and war – often caused by evil people. Most people are aware of the terrible atrocities that have happened in countries such as Bosnia, Sudan, Kuwait and, of course, Tibet. But

---

[4] This event is known as the Parinirvana or final passing into Nirvana. The Buddhists teach that there are altogether 31 different planes of existence, divided into 3 realms. The first and lowest levels are of desire and include humans, animals, demons, hells and spirits of the dead (*pretas*). Above this are six different levels of gods and above this too exist increasingly rarefied forms of gods. Beyond these are the formless realms that are impossible to describe in terms of existence as we know it. Nirvana is beyond even these exalted states.

aside from the self-inflicted suffering of humankind even nature seems to be powered by suffering. Evolution is brutally cruel, wiping out whole species in its quest for advancement. Animals prey on one another; germs mutate to create new ingenious pestilence; natural disasters occur through no one's fault. We, too, are subject to these same laws. Nothing lasts, everything decays, everything is subject to change.

Depressing isn't it? According to Shakyamuni Buddha, all normal life is unsatisfactory but it would be wrong to pessimistically say that all life is suffering. Shakyamuni Buddha is being realistic: the acceptance of the existence of suffering is the essential first step in finding its cause and cure. The remaining three Noble Truths offer this cure.

The second Noble Truth – The Origin of Suffering is Egotistical Desire and Craving (Samudaya)

Most Westerners are brought up to believe that to be happy we must grab what we want from the world. Selfishness and greed are good; ambition is good. 'Go for it!' urge advertisements. But in a world of constant change in which nothing is fixed and everything is transient our desires are bound to remain unfulfilled. The more we cling to our desires the more we are inevitably bound by them and the more we are bound to experience dissatisfaction and suffering. Shakyamuni Buddha explained that it is precisely our egotistical desire which makes us unhappy. It leads us on an eternal wild goose chase of craving, satisfaction and more craving. It is a circle, a trap.

Fortunately, we can free ourselves from this snare if we simply stop running around in circles. The way to become happier is not to pander to our selfishness, but to transcend it. We lose nothing but our chains when we free ourselves from desire. Instead, we gain release, joy and love. Shakyamuni Buddha went further and explained that we should not only cease craving sensual experience but craving for being (eternal life) and craving for non-being (oblivion). Only by letting go of all three aspects of craving can we escape the cycle of rebecoming (*punabbhava*).

Rebecoming happens from moment to moment. Every action we make has an effect on the next action and so on *ad infinitum*, and reincarnation is the long-term result of this process.

This cycle of craving, samsara, is understood to be the cause of our suffering and karma is the accumulative forces of cause and effect that fuel it. One of Shakyamuni Buddha's insights was to realise that craving and karma lead to constant rebirth. But we can escape.

The third Noble Truth – The Cessation of Suffering Comes with the End of Egotistical Desire (Nirodha)

Shakyamuni Buddha demonstrates to us with the example of his life that it is possible to eliminate suffering. If he can do it, then so can we. Once craving and ignorance are extinguished it brings with it the complete eradication of suffering and is equivalent to the complete self-transcendence of Buddhahood. The Buddhist name for this state where all craving, ignorance and suffering are 'blown out' is *nirvana*. (This is explained earlier in this chapter.) It is a state of existence attainable by every sentient being within this life or in lives to come. The liberated person, who has realised this state, may look physically just like any other person except their mind is in another exalted state of consciousness, unruffled by suffering yet still feeling all the pains and pleasures of other human beings. He has transcended pleasure and pain, forever centred in the infinite.

The fourth Noble Truth – The Eightfold Path (Magga)

The fourth Noble Truth expounded by Shakyamuni Buddha gives us practical ways to enable us to gain enlightenment. To realise Nirvana is like waking up to something so obvious that you feel you have known it all along. It's so simple that it escapes us. Shakyamuni Buddha gave us practical ways to bring us back to this, our spiritual birthright in a series of methods called 'The Noble Eightfold Path.' It is this 'middle way' between extremes that leads to the cessation of suffering.

They are:

1 Right vision Sometimes translated as 'right understanding' this path means having the right outlook on life and accepting Shakyamuni Buddha's analysis of human existence. It is the first of the paths in recognition of the fact that we have to have intuitively felt the prompting of our heart telling us that something more satisfying lies beyond our normal experience.

2 Right intention Sometimes translated as 'thought' or 'resolve' this branch means that we have the right attitude to life and see our goal as enlightenment. With this comes our surrender to the unselfish love for all beings. This way and the others that follow are sometimes called the 'Path of Transformation' as they represent the way by which we change ourselves in the light of the vision of truth. This is the basis of all Buddhist ethics in which actions are judged not by a set of rules but by intention.

3 Right speech This and branches four and five that follow refer to moral behaviour. Speech is one of the easiest ways to harm another person. It is also the simplest way to help someone. Furthermore, it can also be a way of wasting energy in idle chatter, gossip, lies or a relentless internal dialogue. Control speech and we begin to control ourselves. Shakyamuni Buddha often stressed the spiritual value of silence.

4 Right action The basic moral code of Buddhism is enshrined in five precepts; to avoid killing, stealing, false speech, sexual misconduct and intoxication. To achieve perfect action (or conduct) the adept must take personal responsibility for their actions and help ever but harm never.

5 Right livelihood Finding the right livelihood in modern society is becoming ever more difficult but it *is* possible to earn a living without harming other beings. Sometimes this requires a major change of lifestyle. In my own case, I gave up a lucrative advertising business in order to make a living in a more ethical way. A Buddhist would certainly think twice about becoming a butcher, arms dealer or publican. All forms of exploitation and greed should be avoided. In Tibet, prior to the communist invasion, the monks would leave the earnings of 'livelihoods' to the lay people. Even agriculture was forbidden in case it harmed small creatures. For example, if monks work the land or build the foundations to a building every square inch of soil had to be sifted to ensure that not a single worm was hurt.

6 Right effort This is the beginning of direct work upon oneself by becoming aware of the good and bad traits in one's personality. The effort is directed to oneself in order to overcome and eliminate the negative aspects of oneself and cultivate one's good qualities. It is not a repressive regime of self-denial but the middle way between the extremes of asceticism and indulgence. Buddhists, and the Tibetan people in particular, are a very gentle people.

7 Right awareness Sometimes translated as mindfulness, this branch teaches the deliberate cultivation of calm and awareness. As well as within the feelings and thoughts, this calm must extend to one's own body and sensations. In this way the Buddhist gains mastery over all of his impulses.

8 Right samadhi Samadhi is a difficult word to translate into Western languages. Sometimes this eighth branch is called 'right concentration' but this misses many important aspects of the word samadhi. It is sometimes used to mean concentration but it can also mean meditation and even the exalted meditative state at the threshold of enlightenment. Samadhi is more than just the method; it points to the fruits of meditation and the goal of the Noble Eightfold Path which is enlightenment.

The Four Noble Truths are the essence of Shakyamuni Buddha's teaching and lie at the heart of every Buddhist tradition in all the countries where Buddhism has taken root. In addition to the above, Shakyamuni Buddha taught that a human being is made up of five categories of elements:

- **Form**—the physical elements that make up the human body
- **Sensation**—the feelings we have as a result of the senses interacting with the material world
- **Perception**—what we become aware of as a result of the senses reacting with the material world
- **Impulses**—the inner will

- **Consciousness**–the awareness of being alive and having thoughts and feelings.

These five elements are all impermanent and constantly changing. They are the five things that make up every human being. Nothing else exists and, in particular, there is nothing corresponding to the concept of 'soul' or 'self'. This belief is one of the main things that differentiates Buddhists from Hindus who believe in a divine self called *atman* which is eternal, unchanging and not dependent on the body or the environment. The atman is in many ways a similar concept to the western 'soul'. Yoga, meditation techniques or a guru can free the atman from bondage to the material plane and allow it to merge with the infinite. Shakyamuni Buddha pointed out that nothing can be found in experience that corresponds to the concept. The 'self' corresponds only to the current state of our ever-changing psychophysical personality. It is an illusion and does not exist as an entity in itself.

Tibetan Tantric Buddhism

The above teachings are the essence of Buddhism but these ideas evolved and changed as they encountered different cultures. In India, Buddhism grew into a major religion but by the twelfth century CE it had almost disappeared in India. This was mainly due to military conquest by the Muslims and the fact that Buddhism was so similar to Hinduism that it was absorbed into it. Elsewhere, Buddhism flourished, spreading far beyond the limits of the Indian subcontinent. By the third century BCE it became the official religion of Sri Lanka, and from there it spread south and east into Thailand, Burma, Cambodia and Indonesia. Later it was to spread throughout China and from there into Korea, Mongolia, Vietnam, Japan and Tibet. Today there is a growing interest in the West and within most countries throughout the world.

Early in its history Buddhism became divided into various different schools. By about the first century CE two main branches of Buddhism had evolved. The more conservative branch, now known as the Theravada school or 'Way of the

Elders', bases its teaching on what is recorded in the Pali Canon and is close to the original teachings of Shakyamuni Buddha.

The other main branch is called Mahayana Buddhism whose followers are much more willing to adapt their teachings and practices to suit different circumstances, cultures and personality types. The Mahayana Buddhists explored the philosophical implications of Shakyamuni Buddha's message and introduced forms of practice which were suitable for the lay people as well as for monks. Shakyamuni Buddha's message of compassion towards all living things and selfless, loving action became their touchstones.

The spiritual goal of the Mahayana Buddhists is not only to seek one's own salvation but to return from this state of bliss to help everyone. This compassionate desire to help all life inevitably arises on realisation of nirvana. This spiritual ideal was called, in Sanskrit, the *bodhisattva* which you read about in Chapter 1. The selfless ideal of the bodhisattva can be applied to both the search for enlightenment for the benefit of all and also to the everyday life of the lay people.

In short, the bodhisattva is one who has vowed to aim at the supreme and perfect enlightenment of Buddhahood in order to save all beings. He, or she, is a hero who has embraced wisdom and compassion, accepted suffering and taken the vow to 'obtain supreme and perfect enlightenment, promote the good of all beings and establish them in the final and complete nirvana – the same vow that the future Shakyamuni is said to have made before Buddha Dipankara in the presence of the heavenly Buddhas.

Furthermore the bodhisattva must practise six perfections (virtues) to attain enlightenment: giving, morality, patience, vigour, meditation and wisdom. Sometimes a further four perfections are spoken of: skill in means, vows, strength and knowledge. Of these, 'skill in means' is the most important as it enables the bodhisattva to always know the right thing to do to help being towards enlightenment in any given circumstances.

Tibetan Buddhists believe, like all Buddhists, in the Four Noble Truths, the three marks of life, karma, rebirth, enlightenment and compassion all of which are firmly rooted in the original teachings (Dharma) of Shakyamuni Buddha. Tibetans are Mahayana Buddhists and accept the idea of the bodhisattva as well as the philosophies of 'emptiness' and 'mind only'. In addition, they are influenced by *tantra* which will be discussed later.

Mahayana Buddhists also accept one or more scriptures as the word of Shakyamuni Buddha. They speak about Buddhas and bodhisattvas such as Avalokitesvara, Manjusri, Maitreya, Kshitigarbha and Tara as being heavenly beings who can be called upon in times of need. Even Shakyamuni Buddha is believed by some to be available in a heavenly form[5]. The Mahayana universe is multi-dimensional with three main realms of sense–desire, form and formlessness, and other worlds in which dwell many Buddhas. The most important Mahayana texts include the *Heart Sutra* (known as *The Heart of Wisdom* in Tibet) in which Avalokitesvara, the Bodhisattva of Compassion, explains that all things, including the five *skandhas* of form, feeling, perceptions, impulses and consciousness, do not exist as separate entities but are all emptiness. The religious Tibetans all know this by heart and chant it solemnly at the beginning of every ceremony. As well as a means of enlightenment, they consider it the most powerful exorcism, purifier and developer of merit and wisdom. The other great text, the *Diamond Sutra*, expands the idea and explains that nothing possesses its own being or has absolute, self-reliant, inherent existence. In other words, nirvana and samsara are empty of inherent existence. There is no essential difference between them as there is no essence to either.

The Tibetan monks follow the *vinaya* rules as passed down by non-Mahayana traditions and in particular the vinaya of the Mulasarvastivadins. One of the main differences is that the Theravada have 227 rules whereas the Mulasarvastivadin have 258. The Mahayanas also believe in *upaya kausalya* (skilful means)

---

[5] The Lotus Sutra claims that Shakyamuni Buddha still lives and works for beings. His birth, death and enlightenment were *upaya* – i.e. 'skilful means', the ability to know exactly what to do for the best in all situations.

whereby teachings and practices are skilfully adapted to the circumstances in order to best help beings make spiritual progress.

From approximately 500 CE a third major branch of Buddhism emerged in India which was to have a profound effect upon Tibetan beliefs. The *Vajrayana*, the Diamond Vehicle', is also sometimes called Tantric Buddhism. Vajrayana is a name often used to distinguish Tantric Buddhism from other forms of Mahayana and is sometimes applied loosely to the whole of Tibetan Buddhism. The word *tantra* comes from a verb meaning 'to weave' and a noun meaning 'thread'. In religion it refers to the technique of spiritual practice in which the ordinary world is joined to the divine by weaving an enlightened universe in place of the realm of suffering. It can also refer to a set of texts that describe these methods.

The Tibetan Tantric system uses a range of powerful symbols and rites to release the latent energies of the individual and propel them towards enlightenment. This method involves the physical body, the emotions, the imagination and the intellect and is shrouded in mystery with strange cryptic texts and secret initiations. Tantric Buddhism lays particular stress on the importance of individual tuition and empowerment from a master or guru. It is very much an 'esoteric' tradition and, as you read earlier, the master-pupil relationship between Marpa and his disciple Milarepa is a good example of this. Tantric Buddhism for centuries was taught as an oral tradition involving secret initiations and cryptic language.

This path is not for the faint-hearted. Practitioners require strong self-control and a highly compassionate attitude. In the wrong hands it can be a dangerous set of techniques and consequently Vajrayana teachers traditionally choose their disciples very carefully. Pure motive and a selfless compassion are required of the disciple who hopes to release and control these powerful energies in the advanced student.

In particular, Tibetan Tantric Buddhism uses 'visualisation' techniques and involves vividly imagining a chosen Buddha or bodhisattva until it appears before the meditator. This being is worshipped and acts as a guide and mentor. Sins are confessed and vows offered to this figure. Practised under close supervision this is a very powerful and beneficial technique but in the wrong hands can be dangerous.

An interesting example of the potential danger of these magical arts is the ability of a meditator to create a phantom being called a *tulpa*. This mind-forged phantom being can sometimes take on a life of its own and even get out of its master's control and become mischievous or even dangerous. The extraordinary British woman traveller Alexandra David-Neel, in her book *Magic and Mystery in Tibet,* describes how she was shown how to create one of these beings by following prescribed visualisation rituals given to her by a lama.

She imagined a harmless character, a short, fat monk 'of an innocent and jolly type'. After several months' concentration and ritual she succeeded in creating the phantom monk' and came to regard him as a guest. He became like a real person but eventually ran out of control and changed into a character with a mocking and malignant look.

It took her a further six months of concentration, meditation and ritual to get rid of the phantom. Later she said of her experience: 'There is nothing strange in the fact that I may have created my own hallucination. The interesting point is that in these cases of materialisation, others see the thought-forms that have been created.'

It is my belief that sometimes the spirit rappings of ouija boards and table tilting from the seance rooms of the West may generate similar self-perpetuating thought forms that we can misinterpret as being real spirits.

In addition to visualisation techniques, Tibetan Tantric Buddhism employs a range of practices as aids towards enlightenment. These include *mantras* (a repetitive form of chanting), *mandalas* (circular designs which are symbolic depictions of the universe), *mudras* (symbolic shapes made by the hands), *yoga* and the sacramental use of sexuality.

Death, Reincarnation and the Dalai Lamas

Buddhism teaches that the energy produced by the mental, emotional and physical activities of a being bring about the reappearance of new mental and physical phenomena after the death of the physical body. According to Buddhism, it is not a soul that reincarnates but rather a set of tendencies that progress onward to enlightenment. But the Tibetan Buddhists have a number of subtle theories about this subject that differ somewhat from the traditional Buddhist beliefs of the Southern orders based in Sri Lanka, Burma and Thailand.

The Tibetan general populace repeat the Buddhist orthodox creed that says '*All aggregates are impermanent*' and *no "ego" exists in the person, nor in anything.*' However, probably because of the powerful influence of Bön, many Tibetans retain the belief that a unified entity leaves the body after death, travelling from world to world and assuming various forms. Southern Buddhists also say that rebirth is instantaneous whereas the Tibetan Lamists affirm that a certain time elapses between death and rebirth.

Tibetans also believe that rebirth can occur into any one of six kinds of recognised sentient beings. These include gods (*lha*), non-gods – a kind if Titan always at war with the gods (*lhamayin*), men (*mi*), animals (*tudo*), non-men – hungry ghosts that forever seek food and water but which always turn to fire whenever they come near (*Yidag* or *mi-ma-yin*[6]) and, finally, the dwellers in purgatories. Common folk also believe that the recitations of *Aum mani padme hum* will assure them a happy rebirth in *Nub Dewa chen*, the Western Paradise of the Great Bliss. According to popular belief, the order of beings in which one is reborn and the circumstances in which one will find oneself in are dependent upon the good and evil deeds done in a previous existence.

But, according to the Tibetans, rebirth is not just a result of accumulated karma. A person who knows the proper methods (*thabs*) is capable of directing his post-mortem destiny. He can use 'skilful means' to be reborn in more agreeable circumstances than if left to chance alone. The burden of past karma will bear a

---

[6] Included in this class are demigods, genii and good and bad spirits of various kinds.

considerable force on the spirit's progress after life and a miserable birth may result, but, nonetheless, the Tibetans believe that the advanced lama can guide his soul to a better life. Dying well is a continuation of the process of living well.

The Tibetans do not necessarily believe that the personality continues after death. The personality disintegrates but what endures is the consciousness or 'the will to live'. At the time of death the lama will be aware of the disintegration of his present personality but will not be troubled. He would have travelled this road before during his meditations and will be able to keep his consciousness fully awake and lucid. It follows that such a man does not need the help of anyone in his final hours and requires no religious rites afterwards to help guide him.

I have to say that as a practising medium I disagree with the Tibetans on this point. In my own spiritual work, evidence has convinced me, and it has been proven to me by others, that the human personality survives death without disintegrating. Also the well reported cases of people who have had a near death experience (NDE), in which they've been temporarily brain dead, bear out the fact that the personality survives death. Many of this evidence has been collected by Elizabeth Kübler-Ross and Raymond Moody. Their studies indicate that there is 'life after life' and that the human identity somehow survives.

My own experience of mediumship has shown that even the irritating idiosyncrasies of personality survive. However, in many ways my beliefs are not far removed from the Lamist's ideas. Many mediums believe that the ultimate goal of the spirit is to merge with the infinite, that after a period in the afterlife the soul incarnates[7], and that the good and bad deeds done on earth affect the progress of the soul.

The Tibetans also have their own NDE cases. They call them *delogs*, which means 'one who has returned from the beyond'. As with western NDE cases they vary in their descriptions of what awaits us in the afterlife but agree in the way the feelings of pseudodeath are depicted as positively pleasant. The Tibetans also

---

[7] Spiritualists do not generally believe in reincarnation. However, a French splinter branch, called Spiritism and founded by Allan Kardec in 1856, believes in reincarnation. It is still a powerful movement throughout the world, particularly within South America.

have their equivalent of our mediums called *pawos*. Some of the descriptions of the states of afterlife that we receive from Western travellers in Tibet tell of how the pawos observes that sometimes the spirits of the dead are disorientated and do not realise that they are dead. They may hover over their physical body and see the lamas chanting around him. (Similar descriptions of earthbound spirits can be found in the records of Spiritualism.) In cases such as this, the disincarnate spirit is encouraged to go to a sandy spot and observe its body's footprints on the ground. If they are reversed to the way the body is standing then it is most definitely dead.

Interestingly, the Tibetans, like Spiritualists, believe in an etheric body, a duplicate body of light that is attached to the physical by means of a silver cord. The Tibetans also believe that the 'ethereal double' can, under certain circumstances, separate from the physical and show itself in different places and travel the world and the subtle planes. The Tibetans believe that trained adepts can achieve this at will and tell of their journeys into paradises, purgatories or the intermediary regions where spirits wander after death. This ethereal double can survive the disintegration of the corpse.

The most important Tibetan Buddhist text that covers the important subject of what lies beyond death is *Bardo Thodol* better known as *The Tibetan Book of the Dead*. *Bardo* means 'intermediate state' and denotes the period which lies between the death of a person and his or her rebirth. *Thodol*, pronounced Thos Grol, means 'liberation through understanding'. The *Bardo Thodol* is a 'treasure text' which is attributed to Padmasambhava (Guru Rimpoche). They remain hidden for centuries and only when humans have progressed enough spiritually to understand them do they reappear. The Tibetan Buddhists believe that there are many such 'treasure texts' and that many more will be rediscovered as humankind becomes more spiritually aware.

According to the *Bardo Thodol,* we can divide our existence into four interlinked realities: life, dying and death, after death and rebirth. These are called the four bardos: the natural bardo of this earthly life, the painful bardo of dying, the luminous bardo of dharmata and the karmic bardo of becoming. As you can see, the bardos embrace the whole of existence and therefore this treasure text is not only about the world after death but is a treatise for this life also. Many lamas will occupy themselves with the writings of the *Bardo Thodol* throughout their lives and not just at the time of death.

The Nirvana that Shakyamuni Buddha realised lies beyond both life and death yet embraces both. Within the inspiring text of the *Bardo Thodol* we read of how to focus the spirit on to this divine essence. By embracing death in the same way we embrace life, we may achieve the same understanding as the Tibetan poet Milarepa: 'My religion is to live— and die— without regret.'

The rebirths of the Dalai lama

According to the Tibetan Buddhists, a person at the time of death will see various visions of 'peaceful' and 'terrifying' beings. They may also see the 'primal light' and may at this precious moment be able to enter Nirvana. However, most people are still entangled in the coils of their karma and will be drawn back into the 'gloomy light' of earthly rebirth. Very few can escape the iron grip of karma and are consequently guided by their *yidams*[8] (guardian spirits) to a new life.

Ideally, the departing soul exits the physical body by the top of the head so that the awareness can progress unhindered. The advanced soul can guide its own progress through the bardos that await it. Some bodhisattvas may deliberately choose a favourable human birth in order to continue their work and help suffering beings. They may even announce before they die the likely place they will be born.

This remarkable idea is fundamental to Tibetan religious society. For example, the master Gendun Drubpa (1391–1474) was a great teacher and founded the Tashi Lhunpo Monastery in Southern Tibet. After his death he was reborn as the son of a

---

[8] The *yidams*, like the peaceful and terrifying being, are all considered to be generated by the dying person's own depths.

yogin and yogini couple and given the name Gendun Gyatso. As soon as he could talk he announced that he was Gendun Drubpa and wanted to be returned to the monastery he founded. He also remembered many other pervious other lives including his incarnation before this as Dromtonpa, the disciple of Atisha.

In his next reincarnation he was called Sonam Gyatso (1543–88) during the height of the Mongolian empire that dominated the region at that time. The ferocious Mongol king Altan Khan, who would think nothing of killing for sport, was so impressed by Sonam Gyatso that he converted to Gelug Buddhism (yellow hats) and renounced his evil ways. Altan Khan bestowed upon Sonam Gyatso the title Dalai Lama, translating literally from the Mongol word as 'Ocean of wisdom'. The title was retrospectively attributed to the first and second Gelugpa heirachs who followed from the tradition's founder Tsongkhapa (1357–1419). Sonam Gyatso became known as His Holiness the third Dalai Lama.

Not only are the Dalai Lamas considered the reincarnations of these fifteenth-century holymen but are also though of as earthly forms of the heavenly bodhisattva Avalokitesvara[9]. (A bodhisattva in human form, taking several rebirths which can be identified is known as a *tulku*.) In Tibet there are also many other recognised lines of incarnations, such as the Panchen Lamas, but all are secondary to the great spiritual lineage of the Dalai Lama.

Prior to his death, a Dalai Lama will give general indications as to the location of his next rebirth. Soon after he dies, a search is made across Tibet for a baby born after the Dalai Lama's death. The rebirth does not necessarily take place at the moment of the predecessor's death and years may pass before the next incarnation is identified.

When a likely candidate is found, the young tulku is tested to see if he really is the reincarnated soul that they seek. The child may recognise old friends, pick out his prayer beads or personal objects from an assortment of similar objects. Sometimes omens are recognised, marks are seen in the landscape or lamas have

---

[9] In Tibetan, *Chen re zi*.

dreams that direct them to the object of their search. Young tulkus are taken from their families and brought up as monks. In most cases, the families are poor and, although the parents may bemoan the loss of a son, they too would be brought to Lhasa and share to a lesser extent in the benefits of the holy bodhisattva lineage. All parental responsibilities and education would be left in the control of the monks.

With Mongol support, the fifth Dalai Lama, Ngawang Lopsang Gyatso (1617–82), became the political leader of Tibet. He founded the Ganden Phodrang Government that Tibetans still consider their legitimate government today. Known as the Great Fifth, he built the famous Potala palace in Lhasa, established the centrality of the monastic institutions, a bureaucratic government and more or less abolished the army. Tibet's historic Chinese enemy under the leadership of the Manchu emperor, fearing Tibet's close ties with the Mongol Empire, recognised the Dalai Lama's secular authority over Tibet and his spiritual authority over the world.

The Dalai Lamas ruled for over 300 years. Sometimes during the eighteenth and nineteenth centuries, the Dalai Lamas were entangled in political intrigue and some may have been assassinated. The thirteenth Dalai Lama (1878-1933) was much loved by Westerners visiting Tibet in the 1920s and 1930s and is recorded as having tried to introduce selective aspects of Western civilisation and technology. Some time before his death in 1933 the thirteenth Dalai Lama had given intimations regarding the manner of his rebirth. After his death, the body was put into a sitting position facing towards the south, as is the custom when a Dalai Lama dies.

One morning it was discovered that the dead body had moved in the night and now its head was pointing towards the east. The State Oracle was urgently summoned and this entranced monk indicated that the new Dalai Lama was to be found in the east. Later, the Regent went on a pilgrimage to the famous holy lake, Chö Khor Gye, and gazed into its mirror waters. It is said that anyone who does this can see into the future. The Regent saw a three-storey monastery with golden roofs, near which stood a little Chinese peasant house with carved gables. Soon the whole nation became alive with speculation as preparations were made to search for the Holy Child.

After a prolonged search, Kyetsang Rimpoche and his delegation in search of the reborn leader of their nation reached the district of Ambo in the Chinese province of Chinghai. It was from this same area that the great reformer of Lamanism, Tsong Kapa, had been born long ago. At last they found the same buildings as seen in the Regent's lake vision. Full of excitement, the monks changed into the clothes of their servants and entered the house where they hoped to find the Holy Child.

As soon as they entered the building, a two-year-old boy ran out to meet them and hugged the Lama who wore around his neck the rosary of the thirteenth Dalai Lama. The boy called out 'Sera Lama', recognising him not only as a lama but also the monastery from which he came. The boy was then given the tests to see if he was indeed the Incarnation. He correctly identified his own rosary from a selection, his drums which his last incarnation had used to call servants and his old walking stick. When they examined his body they discovered all the correct feature and birth marks that should indicate him to be the correct person. These include large outstanding ears and moles on the trunk which are supposed to be traces of the four-armed god's second pair of arms.

The delegation sneaked the child and his parents past the Chinese officials and back to Lhasa where the child was officially greeted as the next Dalai Lama. The child was filled with dignity and grace and greeted many of the monks and his predecessor's servants with such a familiarity as if he had known them for years. Six years had passed since the thirteenth Dalai Lama had died. In February 1940 the enthronement of the Dalai Lama was celebrated during the Great New Year Festival.

Tibet was once a unique and holy country, politically stable with each member of society working towards the goal of enlightenment. As a nation she had all the attributes of independent statehood recognised under international law including a defined territory, a population inhabiting that territory, a government and the ability to enter into international relations. But as the modern era dawned everything in Tibet was to change beyond recognition. Terrible things happened, and still happen, in Tibet. And the world turns its back.

Our present Dalai Lama, the fourteenth, was only 16 years old when the Chinese invaded Tibet in 1951. Already the monks had seen dark omens that warned of disaster. On 15 August 1950, a violent earthquake caused a panic in the Holy City of Lhasa. A large cloud of red dust appeared in the east and there was extensive catastrophe throughout Tibet. Many monks were buried alive in their rock monasteries and it is said that in places the earth opened up and swallowed many people. One morning the capital of the stone column at the foot of the Potala palace was found lying on the ground smashed into fragments. There were many other evil portents of disaster such as deformed animals being born and, to the terror of Lhasa's citizens, water began to flow from a gargoyle on a building despite the dry summer weather. These were terrible omens. Lhasa became alive with gongs, prayers and chanting.

The fall of Tibet

In 1949, Chinese troops began training in mountain warfare. On 7 October 1950, the Chinese advance got underway and within four days had reached Chamdo, a regional capital about 650 kilometres (400 miles) north-east of Lhasa. Tibet mobilised what little forces she had: about 12,000 men armed only with out-of-date British colonial rifles. But this meagrely equipped army knew the terrain and their reputation was always that of fierce, bloody warriors. They prepared to defend the vital city of Chamdo.

Shortly after midnight on 19 October 1950 the sky above Chamdo burst into daylight as the Chinese launched flares. Explosions could be heard. There was panic. Thinking that Chamdo was surrounded and resistance was useless, the Tibetan armies thought it best to retreat and instead defend Lhasa.

The next day, however, they realised that they'd been duped. Chinese spies had infiltrated the town and captured it without firing a shot. What they'd seen and heard were mainly fireworks and other pyrotechnics With the strategic city of Chamdo fallen the People's Liberation Army had no real resistance. Against the advice of the State Oracle the Dalai Lama stayed in Tibet and agreed with the Chinese that Tibet would renounce their independence but keep a certain amount of self-government under the Dalai Lama.

In May 1950 a treaty was imposed on the Tibetan government by the newly established communist government of China. It acknowledged China's sovereignty over Tibet but also recognised the Tibetan government's autonomy with respect to Tibet's internal affairs. As the Chinese tightened their grip upon the nation, they repeatedly violated the treaty. Open resistance against the invaders grew and in 1959 there was a failed National Uprising which resulted in the flight of the Dalai Lama into India where he continues to run a government in exile and make the world aware of the terrible plight of Tibet and the abuse of human rights, the rampant environmental destruction and, in particular, how the influx of millions of Chinese settlers are making the Tibetan people a minority in their own country.

Faced with the terrible destruction of his country, the Dalai Lama still urges his people not to resort to violence to overcome their oppressors. On 10 December 1989 he was awarded the Nobel Peace Prize. The citation read

> *The Committee wants to emphasise the fact that the Dalai Lama in his struggle for the liberation of Tibet consistently has opposed the use of violence. He has instead advocated peaceful solutions based upon tolerance and mutual respect in order to preserve the historical and cultural heritage of his people.*

He accepted the prize on behalf of the people of Tibet but also on behalf of the oppressed everywhere and for all those who struggle for freedom and work for world peace. He said 'The prize reaffirms our conviction that with the truth, courage and determination as our weapons, Tibet will be liberated. Our struggle must remain non-violent and free of hatred.'

Words like these are bringing the essence of Tibet's wisdom to the whole world.

Part 2
TIBETAN WISDOM'S RELEVANCE TODAY

Chapter 3
What can the timeless wisdom of Tibet teach us about about ourselves?

We are looking for happiness in the wrong place. Today people have more material things than ever before yet are terribly insecure. We seek happiness in beautiful surroundings, expensive cars, fine clothes and food. We try to secure our future with life assurance and medical cover. We hope that our jobs will remain secure, that our marriages will last and that illness will not strike our family. But none of these things can bring lasting happiness. Everything we own and the lifestyle we maintain are only temporary. They are terribly frail things that give us no protection from the blows of destiny. They are all outside of ourselves and subject to decay. They should not be our refuge.

We may accumulate wealth, property, fame and knowledge but what will protect us when death approaches? It may come in many years' time or be in the next few moments. A wise man does not cling to the external world for he knows that one day he must leave it. Every day could be his last.

Only a few have realised that consistent happiness can be achieved by progressing spiritually. The treasure of happiness lies not outside but within the human heart. It manifests as compassion and wisdom. Shakyamuni Buddha's story and the stories of all the Tibetan saints illustrate that this inner journey is the most important part of a person's life. The people we read about who pioneered this path are mainly ordinary men and women from poor families. They discovered treasures more precious than anything that the world can offer. Collectively, the people of Tibet raised the consciousness of their nation and now stand as an example of spirituality and courage in the face of adversity. Their strength as a nation and their ability to endure such hardship and humiliation comes from the fact that, despite what the Chinese invaders may inflict, the people and their spiritual leaders remain focused on the light that shines within. This alone is stronger than external fate.

Every one of us will, in this life or lives to come, also take this spiritual journey, for spiritual evolution is forever heavenwards. As the Japanese Zen Buddhists say 'one day even the grass will be enlightened'. But who takes this spiritual journey? Who is this person that I call 'I'? What is a person? What is a self? To truly know the answer to these questions is the goal of the inner quest. It is a journey from you to you.

What we perceive as the 'I' changes from moment to moment. A man at 70 is not the boy he was at 10, yet between the two points in time there is a continuity of consciousness. Our true self is the consciousness which transcends identity and memory. According to the Tibetan Buddhists, when ignorance and craving are overcome by the Great Awakening of Buddahood and when nirvana is attained, then the personal consciousness is realised to have been an illusion. Like time and space, the self is only a relative and not absolute existence. So just as we cannot find happiness in the things of the world so, too, we cannot find happiness if we cling to any illusion of self.

Shakyamuni Buddha emphasised that the objective of human existence is to attain 'Deliverance of the Mind' which, in effect, means the transcendence of the illusionary mundane mind and realisation of the supramundane mind which is unborn. To know this unshaped being is to realise the state of enlightenment. Shakyamuni Buddha said:

> *And therefore, ye disciples, the gain of the Holy Life is neither alms, nor honour, nor fame, neither the virtues of the Order, nor the bliss of samadhi, nor clearness of insight, but*

the fixed, unalterable Deliverance of the Mind. This, ye disciples, is the purpose of the Holy Life; this is its central core; this is the goal.
(Majjhima-Nikaya, Maha-Saropama Suttra)

Illustration

The 'I' is empty of inherent existence

Usually phenomena are divided into two types: (a) the mental and physical things that are used by the 'I'; (b) the I that uses them. When someone calls my name to what are they referring? For example, when someone calls out to me 'Hello Craig', are they referring to my body? No, clearly my body is not the thing that is me. Similarly, it is not my mind, for both mind and body are things used by me. Neither is the 'I' itself. There is clearly an 'I' that is separate from the mind and body. Mind and body are things that I use, they are not the essential me.

I may complain about my body if it gets ill or I may reprimand my mind if it loses concentration or cannot recall a memory. If I cut my fingernails am I throwing away part of myself? Think about your own concept of 'I'. What is its nature? Does your 'I' have a separate identity from your mind and body? Notice how the more you search for the 'I' the more elusive it is. It is impossible to pin down. The Tibetan Buddhists teach us that the seemingly independent 'I' doesn't exist at all. This specific non-existence is what the Tibetan Buddhists refer to as selflessness. The 'I' is an illusion.

The ultimate nature of the 'I' is emptiness. The 'I' is empty of inherent existence as, too, are all things used by it. The 'I' and the things used by the 'I' are, therefore, the same. There is no difference between you and that. If the mind dwells on the meaning of emptiness, the dualistic division of things becomes less. The meditator may see all things including himself or herself as the one clear light.

Tibetan Buddhists do not say that there is a self that is completely separate from the mind and body. They say that there is no permanent independent self. Buddhism says that the following truths hold good that: (a) all things are impermanent; (b) all conditioned things are liable to suffering; (c) all phenomena are empty of self; (d) nirvana is peace.

Application

Fixing the mind in meditation

A tremendously important part of all Buddhist philosophy is the stress it places on meditation as the way to salvation. In the West, we have access to so many different systems that it can be confusing to know where to start. We not only have all the many Buddhist forms available to us but there are the systems to be found in yoga, Hinduism, Theosophy, Spiritualism, Taoism, New Age, etc. This is not a bad thing. The Tibetan Buddhists themselves have thousands of meditation techniques. Each has a different objective and different styles suit different types of personality. But from a Buddhist perspective the ultimate goal of all meditation is to travel beyond the 'I' into the great immensity called nirvana.

To practise even a little meditation can bring great benefit to you. From a practical standpoint you will gain greater vitality, mental alertness and health but most importantly you will gain the inner treasure of peace. This, in turn, will inevitably improve your relations with others, hopefully increase your compassion and make you a better and more stable person. On a more subtle level, you are making tremendous progress spiritually and may bring yourself great merit that will serve you well in future lives. And your progress will become even more advanced when you perceive meditation not as a means of self gain but as something that is of benefit to all beings. When meditation becomes a form of service for the sake of all beings then you have put your foot on the bodhisattva's road.

A Tibetan Buddhist respects the various meditation techniques of the different systems within and outside Buddhist tradition. As with most meditation practices, the Tibetans advise that it is best to practise meditation in a quiet place during the morning when the mind is clear and alert.

The meditation experiment that follows is a traditional and widespread Tibetan technique used to fix the concentration. Although it is, in itself, simple, some of the Tibetan adepts used variations on this method to develop the most advanced systems.

1 First, you must make yourself comfortable. Sit on a chair or on the floor if you can. Arrange your legs in the most comfortable position and make your backbone as straight as an arrow. Place your hands in the meditative equipoise at about 5cm (2 inches) below the navel, left hand at the bottom and right hand on top with your thumbs touching to form a triangle. Your hands are now in the gesture of meditation. The nerve channel associated with the mind of enlightenment (*Bodhichitta*) passes through the thumbs. Thus, joining of the two thumbs in this gesture is of auspicious significance for the future development of the mind of enlightenment. Furthermore, this placement of the hands has connection with the place inside the body where inner heat is generated.

2 Now bend your neck down slightly. Let the top of your tongue touch the roof of your mouth near the top of your teeth. In some Tibetan practices the eyes are focused on the tip of the nose but for this exercise let your eyes gaze gently downwards. Gaze without straining towards the floor in front of you. Do not open your eyes wide, rather let the lids relax. Occasionally they may close of their own accord. Do not worry about this; once your mental equilibrium is steady your eyes will fix naturally into the gaze. Be aware of how your mind is becoming quiet and how your breathing is slowing down.

3 Now you will shift the attention away from the mind and meditate on an object of observation. In Tibetan meditative techniques these can be external or internal. Something with spiritual significance or symbolism can be used in this technique. You can choose any item you wish such as a flower, a cross or perhaps the face of a great spiritual teacher. For this exercise we'll imagine a statue of the Buddha. Visualise that it is about 120 cm (4 feet) in front of you at the same height as your eyebrows. It is about 5cm (2 inches) high and is radiating light. As well as using your visual imagination also conceive of it as being heavy; this will help you to fix the attention further. The heaviness is said to prevent over-excitement and the brilliance of the light will prevent laxity. You have two objectives: (a) make the object of observation clear; (b) make it steady.

4 Observe your thoughts and impressions. Are the things you see with your eyes bothering you? If they are then close your eyes and observe what you see. If you see a reddish colour when your eyes are closed then you are too involved in eye consciousness. Try to withdraw the attention from the eye to the mental consciousness. Your attention should be entirely concentrated on the Buddha that you are visualising.

5 The steadiness of your observation of your Buddha will fluctuate depending upon the excitability of your thoughts. To stop this scattering, withdraw the mind even more within so that the intensity of your thinking begins to lower. To help this process, it is advised that should briefly think about something sombre. These weighty thoughts will slow down the heightened mode of appreciation of the Buddha image you are visualising. This will increase the stability of your mental inner observation.

6 To get the balance right you must also develop clarity. The biggest enemy of this is laxity which can lead to lethargy and the complete loss of the mental image. This is caused by an over-withdrawal of the mind. To stop this, you must raise the mode of appreciation. It is the opposite of what you did in order to get stability of the observation This time you should think of something that makes you feel joyous or exhilarated such as looking at a beautiful scene from the mountain tops. This will lift the mind and heighten its mode of appreciation. You must judge the appropriate times when you need to increase the clarity or stability of your mental picture. Notice how, by controlling your sombre and joyous thoughts, you affect the mental picture that you are creating.

7 Now inspect the mental image of the Buddha that you have created in your mind's eye. Observe it from all angles:

from above, from the corners. Is it both clear and stable? Observing the mental image in this way is called 'introspection' by the Tibetan Buddhists. By learning to do this and controlling the steadiness and clarity of the mental picture you are, at the same time, controlling the mind. When you develop mindfulness, you can catch laxity and excitement of thoughts before they arise and even control when these thoughts arise

The above technique is the classic way a Tibetan monk will sustain meditation using an external object of meditation. In a similar way, the meditator can look at the mind itself. The consciousness will become empty like clear water. It is then at the very heart of observation itself.

Chapter 4

What can the timeless wisdom of Tibet teach us about human relationships and sexuality?

We can meditate all we like, but without compassion in our hearts we will never realise the ultimate truth. All the methods in the world cannot compare to the power of compassion. Without compassion, Tibetan Buddhism is worthless and selfish. Wisdom must be accompanied by the motivation of love.

Loving kindness and compassion, clear-headed and free of emotionalism, can reach even the hardest heart. It can touch the hearts of even your enemies. This is the highest form of love that the Tibetans practise. In response to the Chinese aggressors they offer forgiveness and love. In time, I'm sure Tibet will prove to the world, as Mahatma Gandhi did, that the power that springs from the human heart is greater than the mightiest of empires.

The Tibetans say that love must be unbiased and in-tune with the realisation of reality. Human emotional love is close to attachment and can reach only those people receptive to it such as our parents, friends, wife, husband, children, etc. This sort of love is exclusive. It is biased. It cannot touch the iron-clad hearts of our enemies. Love, kindness and compassion must extend beyond all limitations. It must be inclusive of all. Enlightenment triggers infinite compassion, infinite love, infinite kindness. It is selfless and all embracing.

So, in human relationships we must recognise that there are two manifestations of love. Of course, we must love our partner, friends, family and children but we must also try to expand this compassion if we are to come anywhere close to the teachings and example of Shakyamuni Buddha. One way of doing this is to start with the love and compassion you know and understand and expand this to include everything. You may imagine how your love expands, it surrounds you and your immediate family, expands further to include your friends, your neighbours, your work colleagues, your enemies, your country, your world. Like a spark from a fire, love can set the world aflame. It knows no limit.

Shakyamuni Buddha, the Tibetan saints, his holiness the fourteenth Dalai Lama and every true Tibetan monk always emphasise that compassion lies at the heart of Buddhism. The compassionate person recognises that everyone suffers as much as themselves. Everyone wants happiness and it is their divine birthright to overcome suffering. On this basis a person develops a desire to help others, irrespective of one's attitude to oneself.

Modern life is full of anguish, suffering, fear and anger partly because of the troubles caused by human love. The permissive society has made people much more vulnerable than ever before. Divorce is on the increase and the world is full of the heart-breaking tales of broken families. Shakyamuni Buddha offers us the teachings of compassion, but how can we apply these teachings to the real problems that beset human relationships? Can a religion that mainly practises celibacy and a monastic life ever help solve the emotional problems of ordinary people? And what has a male-dominated religion to say that's helpful to women?

Shakyamuni Buddha's trick was always to look not just at the suffering but to the cause of suffering in order that it can be overcome. The most powerful love is the self-sustaining love that does not try to grasp after the object of its desire. The Tibetan monk and nun are serene in their compassion. Most of the problems of human relationships are caused by possessiveness and power. In many ways, Buddhism and Tibetan Buddhism are male-oriented organisations. Whatever their teachings have to say about human relationships must, of course, apply equally to both sexes.

The ordination of women

After his enlightenment Shakyamuni Buddha, whilst staying at Kapilavastu, was approached by Mahaprajapati, his maternal aunt who had brought him up after his own mother, Mayadevi, had died when he was just a few days old. She made an unprecedented request – could she be ordained and have permission to go forth into the homeless life? Shakyamuni Buddha's response was direct and to the point: 'No!' Mahaprajapati made her request again and three times Shakyamuni Buddha refused her. She was told that she should not even wish for such a thing and she went away in tears.

But Mahaprajapati did not accept Shakyamuni Buddha's refusal to ordain her. Some time later she shaved off her hair, put on saffron robes and together with a number of Shakyan women went to meet Shakyamuni Buddha at Vaisali. She arrived bedraggled from the journey, with swollen feet, weeping and wailing and her eyes filled with tears. She is met by Ananda, Shakyamuni Buddha's constant companion, who takes pity on her. He goes immediately to Shakyamuni Buddha and tells him that Mahaprajapati has made the arduous journey from Kapilavastu and suggests that he should grant her an interview.

Shakyamuni Buddha refuses him three times. But Ananda persists. He asks Shakyamuni Buddha if it is possible for women to follow his teachings and attain the fruits of 'Stream Entry', 'Once Returning', 'Never Returning' or Arahantship (Enlightenment). Shakyamuni Buddha admits that women can, whereupon Ananda reminds him that Mahaprajapati had been like a mother to him even suckling him as her own baby. Would it not be a good thing if women as compassionate as this were to join the order?

Finally, Shakyamuni Buddha relents and accepts Ananda's argument, agreeing that woman are capable of attaining these

Human relationships and sexuality

high ideals. He would allow the ordination of Mahaprajapati but she, and others who follow her, must agree to keep eight rules:

1. No matter how long she's been a nun, she should always bow down to all male monks- even the novice monk.
2. She must never spend the rainy season where there is a monk residing.
3. At the half month she must await the appointing of the *uposatha* (new moon and full moon days) and the coming of a brother to preach the sermon.
4. At the end of keeping the rainy season she must, in the presence of both monks and nuns, invite enquiry of things seen, heard, and suspected.
5. If found guilty of wrong-doing she must do penance for half a month to both Orders.
6. Having passed two seasons in the practice of the above six rules she may ask for full orders from both Orders.
7. She must never abuse or censure a brother monk.
8. She must never speak among the brethren but it is not forbidden for the brethren to speak to her.

Mahaprajapati agreed to Shakyamuni Buddha's rules of conduct.

The main function of the eight rules for women as spoken by Shakyamuni Buddha seem a little unfair and I'm sure would make many a modern woman's blood boil. Clearly, the main purpose of the rules was to keep the nuns subordinate to the monks. Some scholars have suggested that these rules were made in order to prevent a separate order of nuns that would have to be headed by a woman— Shakyamuni Buddha being a man would not easily be seen as the head of a female order. The rules are most likely to have been designed in order to prevent feminism by stopping women from claiming equality with, or superiority over, men.

But these seemingly unjust rules had a specific purpose. Shakyamuni Buddha wanted to prevent women from joining the order for the wrong reasons. For example, a woman might seek ordination because she wanted to leave her husband, or because she was a widow or because she wanted to gain social status. Her parents may have been unable to find her a husband and she had no means of income or support. Shakyamuni Buddha didn't want his spiritual movement to become a welfare organisation. People must join only for spiritual reasons and not to escape social problems. The eight strict rules were put in place to ensure that Mahaprajapati chose this path purely for spiritual reasons. And, of course, this sincerity of motivation must apply equally to men.

Women and Tibet

Amongst Buddhists the interpretation of Shakyamuni Buddha's rules for women is often a subject of heated debate, particularly as many Western women are now being ordained. Many are upset by the gender discrimination within the Tibetan religious institutions. The monk's advantages within the Tibetan community in India are still apparent: they receive better education, more financial support and greater respect than the nuns. However, in the West this inequality is being eroded and Tibetan Buddhism is experiencing a rapid modernisation.

At its worst Tibetan society oppressed women. Men and women were treated very differently in matters of upbringing and education. Even the poorest families would do everything possible to get their sons into a lamasery. Girls were rarely given the opportunity. Common folk's marriages were normally arranged by parents and sometimes the girls were considered as items of trade. A woman's life was often arduous. A large percentage of Tibetan families were polyandrous or polygamous and because such a large proportion of the male population became lamas and not allowed to marry there was also a high proportion of one-parent families. Women had no right of inheritance and no say in the management of the property of the family.

However, if we look at the history of any nation we will soon uncover the same story of female oppression. Certainly the Chinese invaders of Tibet enjoy pointing out the faults of former Tibet. They hail the *Patriotic and Democratic Women's Association of the Tibet Autonomous Region* as the great liberator of women. The truth is that the modern era has seen a tyrannical oppression of Tibetan women by the Chinese that far surpassed any wrongs done in the past. A quote from a news story that appeared in the *Washington Post* about Tibetan political prisoners makes this quite clear:

> 'They beat us with whatever was at their disposal, including wash basins and mugs,' he said. 'They kicked us and used pistol butts and wooden sticks on us.' The released prisoners said that interrogators used electric cattle prods as an instrument of torture. Some prisoners also underwent the 'Chinese Rope torture,' he said. 'I saw people hanging from ropes tied to their arms behind their backs, suspended with their feet off the ground. Two of the people I saw had their shoulders dislocated by the rope. Many became unconscious as a result.' Both former prisoners said that those who were treated most harshly in the prisons were Tibetan nuns. Most of the imprisoned nuns have been released from prison but were said to be reluctant to talk about the experience. (Southerland, 1988)

But perhaps the worst atrocities being committed against Tibetan women are the forced abortions. Blake Kerr is an American physician who visited Tibet and is the author of *Sky Burial*. He spoke with a Tibetan nurse named Chimi:

> 'Tibetan women are allowed to have two children,' Chimi said, 'but if they have one this is considered best… if a woman has a second child, the child will have rights but this is discouraged. Sterilisation is done automatically on many women delivering their second child at Chinese hospitals… In villages there are thousands of illegal children. Tibetans would rather have their own way.' When asked how these children survived, Chimi said that such 'illegal persons' had to do things like collect dung. My stomach felt queasy as Chimi described how 'unauthorised' pregnancies were routinely terminated with lethal injections. Chimi said that she herself had given hundreds of these injections… (Kerr, 93)

Love and compassion

It is so sad to see a society that believed in the power of love and compassion brought to such depths of humiliation. Travellers to Tibet prior to the Chinese invasion describe its people as a happy, mysterious and jolly people. Whatever the faults of the traditional Tibetan system it in no way compares to the dreadful abuse of human rights that is happening today.

In contrast we hear the voice of the Dalai Lama urging all peoples of the world to become more compassionate towards each other. He encourages female rights: 'I think it's very important for women to try to appropriate all their rights. Among the Tibetan refugee community in India, I have for many years been advocating for the female side, the nuns' side. They must have the interest or courage to study as the monks do.' In human relationships he encourages us to take the same selfless attitude towards each other as Shakyamuni Buddha had towards all life. 'Marriage should not be based on blind love or an extreme sort of mad love', says the Dalai Lama, 'it should be based on a knowledge of one another and an understanding that you are suitable to live together. Marriage is not for temporary satisfaction, but for some kind of sense of responsibility. This is the genuine love which is the basis of marriage.'

The Dalai Lama has also spoken out about a number of human relationship issues that affect the modern world. He said of homosexuality: 'It is wrong. Should be avoided'. At another time he said: 'In the name of freedom of sex, then that is included. But at the same time, male and female... has a definite purpose. Not only a few moments' pleasure but reproduction. Life itself. It creates substance. Not other side. No adequate reasons.' About AIDS he says that the disease 'reminds people not to be promiscuous and sexually deviant.' It's not a question of morality or religious acceptance. Sexual freedom has gone too far. 'This disease very much involves sex... or different kinds of sex. So to me, I think people have gone beyond the limits indulging in freedom of sex.'

Illustration

Tantra and human relationships

According to the *Vinaya Vastu,* men and women both have the right to the highest ordination. Everyone has the same Buddha nature which is neither male nor female. However, in advanced texts such as *Abhidharma Kosha* it is assumed that the practitioner is always male. However, from the Tantric Yoga standpoint there is no discrimination between gender. In fact, there are specific precepts for Tantric practitioners which point out that if you belittle a woman it constitutes an breaking of the Tantric precepts.

Tantra is symbolised by sexual union and is, therefore, not complete without the equal participation of both male and female practitioners. The union empowers both parties. Tantric sex is completely different from ordinary sex. The Tibetans believe that both male and female practitioners can become fully enlightened in their forms as male and females. There is so much misconception about Tantra and the use of sexuality as a vehicle to enlightenment that I will not go into detail here. Suffice it to say that Tibetan Buddhism does not prohibit normal sexual relations between people.

One of the most ancient tantric beliefs is that a novice can be 'charged' with divinity through intercourse with an adept of the opposite sex. Some Tantric rituals involve the initiation of a new practitioner by a woman who transmits her potency to him. She would have gained her own power by engaging in sexual intercourse with one or more lamas. Women with the power to create new male Tankrikas are called *dakinis*. Some texts describe how Padmasamdhava, who you remember brought Buddhism to Tibet, gained his power by raping a dakini in her home in a cemetery, then meditating in eight other cremation grounds. (Tankrikas are often instructed to make their homes in graveyards and Tibetan Buddhists would meditate on the female god *Lha-mo* imagining her sitting inside a rotting corpse.) In most cases, the Tantric texts are addressed to men who must awaken their inner feminine energy in order to become whole. In Tibet it is still common practice for a male guru to place a statue of a dakini so that it straddles the lap of a (male) initiate as an act of symbolic, empowering intercourse.

I believe that it is mistaken to believe that celibacy is required for enlightenment but clearly Tantric Buddhism is a minefield when interpreted by Western 'New Age Gurus'. Aleister Crowley used Tibetan and Hindu Tantra as part of his black magic ritual that once so shocked English society. Monks and nuns who practise celibacy do so in order to reduce their desire and attachment to the illusionary. However, in Tantric practices that involve sexual intercourse it is instructed that the sexual energy should never be let out. It must be controlled and eventually returned to other parts of the body. These regenerative fluids can be used to develop bliss as explained in the *Kalachakra* literature.

The same non-emission of semen or sexual 'energy drops' as the Dalai Lama calls it also applies to women. According to the Tibetan beliefs and also the Hindu Tantra systems, the female also has these 'energy drops' which must be conserved. Tantrayana is a yoga aimed primarily at realising enlightenment. Naturally it is easily misunderstood and open to much malpractice— particularly in the West. Tibetan philosophy always urges not to just consider the form but to consider the motives behind our actions. For many people celibacy may be the simplest and easiest way to become free of attachment. For others the practice of Tantra may be a better route. In a general sense we should always apply compassion and sincerity in our sexual relations rather than lust and greed. If we can do this then we may draw a little closer to the ultimate union with nirvana.

APPLICATION

Removing suffering from people you love

In the previous chapter you were shown how to use visualisation to still the mind. Tibetan Buddhism employs thousands of different versions of these visualisation techniques to help you to release yourself and others from suffering and propel you towards enlightenment. In the next exercise you will try a simple technique that I have customised to enable you to improve your relationship with your partner by knowing his or her true nature. I would also highly recommend the book *Taming the Tiger* by Akomg Tulku Rinpoche which looks at techniques similar to these but in much more depth than I have space for here.

You will remember how Chapter 3 you used the power of the mind to visualise a Buddha. By doing this you learnt to still the thoughts and increase your mental inner observation. In this next instance you are going to use your meditation for the benefit of another. Every human relationship includes negative emotions. These bind us, prevent our liberation and limit our spiritual progress. The antidote is compassion. But for the medicine to work it must be used: compassion must be put into practice. One way of doing this is to take on the suffering of others. However, our ordinary human selves would soon become entangled so we must use the invincible power of the transcendent Buddha nature that lies within us all to cut the negative ties that bind us.

1 Make yourself comfortable. Sit on the floor or on a straight-backed chair. Place your hands in the gesture of meditation as you did in Chapter 3. Bend your neck down slightly and let your tongue touch the roof of your mouth near the top of your teeth. Relax. Close your eyes and be aware of how your breathing is slowing down and your mind is becoming still.

2 Consider the proposition that your true nature is fully awakened to the ultimate reality. You are nirvana. At your heart you are enlightened. Spend about five minutes attuning yourself in this way and notice how you feel a deep inner calm.

3 Imagine that the gross mind is falling away from you like unwanted baggage. Let go of the emotions, the worries, the thoughts. As it all falls away into space you see a golden light. It is forming into a ball. It is brilliant and alive. See its radiance, feel its warmth and sense its peace. Now become that ball of light. Be confident that this is your true nature. You are the pure unsullied light of consciousness, without form and void. It is magnificent. It is the pure light of compassion that lies at the heart of all beings. Remain in this state of awareness for about five minutes before moving on to the next stage.

4 You feel clear and alert. Notice how good it feels to be freed from the bondage of your negative emotions and idiosyncrasies. Now turn your attention to the inner

picture of the people you love. See how they are bound by their ignorance. See and feel how their clear light is sullied by the darkness of negative emotion. See how each is bound by suffering. But also feel the joy of knowing that each of them is, like you, the pure light that lies within. You are going to use the power of compassion to remove their suffering. Later you can work on each person separately or together. For this exercise you will focus on your partner.

5 See your partner as a ball of light that is sullied by black patches of imperfection. Without ego you are going to use your breathe to take the darkness from them. As you breath in imagine that you draw in their suffering. It may be emotional, physical, mental. You draw it like a thick black smoke away from them and into yourself.

6 As this dark cloud enters you, see how it merges with the great ball of light that is your light of transcendent wisdom. The negative energy is now transformed by your inner light. The dark smoke becomes living energy. It sparkles and is alive. It makes you feel stronger. You transmute the negative into the positive. Your pure light performs a spiritual alchemy. Every time you breathe in you free your loved ones of their suffering and transform their suffering into light. As you breath out the light is given back to them as compassion. See them become stronger and better people. Do this for three slow breaths and then rest.

7 Repeat stage 6 a few times until you see the darkness lift from your partner. The smoke becomes thinner and weaker and is replaced by good energy. The work has been done. You have helped you partner and also helped yourself in the process. By focusing on the inner light in this way you will not retain any of the negativity that you draw into yourself. Concentrate always on the clarity and beauty of the light. It is always clear and pure. You are the light and cannot suffer harm.

8 Choose a time each day to practise this technique. In the future, you may want to extend your compassion and project it to someone else: a family member, a friend, an animal or even to your worst enemy. The transformative power of compassion knows no limit.

Chapter 5
What can the timeless wisdom of Tibet teach us about children and the family?

As parents we should recognise that the children in our care are not only the product of our genetics but have lived before in other lives. This may be their first human incarnation or they may have lived many previous human incarnations. Indeed, we may have known them before in previous existences and may share a common karma with them. Whatever the spiritual status of our children, we should be aware that this is probably not the first time they've visited this earth. Our responsibility as parents is, therefore, to help our children to rediscover their spiritual nature and establish a moral code and self-discipline with compassion as its touchstone.

There is not a great deal that we can draw from the Tibetan tradition to give us direct guidance about the upbringing of children within a family or by a parent. The written traditions we have are, of course, produced by the monastic organisations that had renounced the worldly ties of family. However, the monks and nuns were responsible for the upbringing of reincarnated lamas given by their families to the monasteries at a very young age. These children would be brought up with great kindness and instructed in the ways of Tibetan Buddhism from early childhood. The Dalai Lama has been asked on a number of occasions about how we should bring up children and, as far as I am aware, he has preferred to steer the debates towards secular issues. On one occasion he was asked 'What are the most important features in bringing up children?' He replied with his characteristic wry smile: 'I think you should ask a specialist. That would be better!'

One interesting point that he and other Tibetan lamas have made is that the education of children begins when the baby is in its mother's womb. The mother's calmness of mind has a positive effect on the unborn child but an angry or negative state of mind can be detrimental to the mind, body and spirit of the unborn child. Scientists would agree. It has been established that the earliest period of a child's life is the most important. The first few weeks after birth are a time when the child's brain is growing rapidly and forming the neurological connections that will set the precedents for his future behaviour and intelligence. During this period, the mother's touch, or someone in the role of a mother, is crucial. The suckling of a new-born child is the perfect way that nature has devised to bond the mother and baby and, if possible, is the best start a baby can expect in life. Suckling creates better health of body, mind and spirit. Without affection at these early stages of life, the child's development will be seriously impeded. In particular, this has been observed in abandoned children such as those from the dilapidated orphanages of war-torn Bosnia. Babies respond to and grow into better people if they know the gentle touch of compassion.

My personal belief is that in all our dealings with people we should always endeavour to communicate with the highest within a person's nature. The same is true when communicating to a child. Talk to children as if speaking directly to the Buddha within them. This is difficult to do for it means that we have first to free ourselves from our own weakness and pettiness that clouds our own Buddha nature. I think of it as God talking to God or perhaps in this context it would be better to say Buddha talking to Buddha. The sentiment is the same.

Education should not so much be about what you put into a person but what you can draw out of them. This becomes particularly relevant when we think about the potential a child may have carried forward with them from their past incarnations. Who knows what we may unlock for the good if we can encourage our children to unlock their latent potential. We must also talk to their Buddha nature and encourage it to flower into wisdom and compassion.

The curious phenomenon of child prodigies may be evidence to show that it is possible to recapture information from forgotten lives. For example, in the eighteenth century Jean Cardiac was able to recite the alphabet when he was only three months old, and could speak his mother tongue, French, aged just one year old. He could converse in Latin at the age of three, in English at four and in Greek and Hebrew at six. In addition he was skilled in many of the arts before dying at the age of seven in 1726. Consider also the case of the 'Infant of Lübeck' in Germany who was born in 1721. He talked within a few hours of his birth, knew the chief events of the early parts of the Bible at the age of one and knew the whole Bible by the age of two. At the age of three he was brought before the King of Denmark who was astonished at the child's knowledge of Latin and French and his extensive knowledge of world history. This child prodigy even appeared to have precognition of the future. He predicted his own death, which occurred when he was four.

These remarkable 'powers' would not surprise a Tibetan Buddhist teacher as they can easily be explained by the theory of reincarnation. A Tibetan Buddhist would recognise such a child as the incarnation of a highly evolved being and train them for a life of spiritual authority. I wonder how Mozart, who could compose at the age of five, would have been treated if he'd been born in Tibet? Or what other great breakthroughs would Pascal have made if he had been trained properly from an early age? He discovered a new geometrical system when he was 11 and wrote a treatise on acoustics at the age of 12. Did these great men, and others perhaps who never rose to fame, carry forward knowledge from their past lives?

Although there are no Tibetan Sutras or manuscripts to specifically guide us with family life and the upbringing of children, you can see how easy it is to apply Tibetan ideas in general to this area of life. The traditional Tibetan family system is, however, something quite alien to our own culture. On the one hand there were millions of monks and nuns living without family ties and at the other extreme was an uneducated peasant class with the extensive practice of polygamy and polyandry. Polyandrous families were usually composed of two or three brothers sharing the same wife. Sometimes the parents who arranged these marriages hoped this would encourage the brothers to live together in harmony. Polyandrous marriages also had the practical function of preventing family estates from being broken up. There were many other practical reasons for this way of life which helped sustain the smooth running of life in this unique country.

Illustration

Tibetan Buddhism and children

What we can apply to modern family life is the wisdom and human values cherished by Tibetan Buddhism in general. To do this we must mobilise the power within ourselves and in the people around us. Parenting is a challenge that may soon upset your equilibrium so it is even more important to apply the meditative practice of patience, forgiveness, letting go, compassion, steadfastness and equanimity to this important part of life. In my own case, I was a single parent for eight years and brought my first daughter up from a baby. At the same time I went through some harrowing financial difficulties and without the sustenance of spiritual practice I don't expect I'd have been able to make it through. Spirituality helps the parents and, of course, the child. It brings peace, happiness and keeps you smiling.

Children have an inherent spiritual dimension to their lives that expresses itself naturally in their play. Meditation is hard for them to understand and may seem to be something foreign and out of context. It is something their parents go away and do. Perhaps the best way we can explain these things to children is to say that meditation is all about being awake in our lives and awake in ourselves. We could also encourage children to reflect upon compassion, or interconnectedness, or to see impermanence and emptiness within their experience.

We may also point out to them the benefits of being attentive. We can teach them to focus their attention on the present or show them how times spent in silence while walking through the woodlands can be a joyful experience. The teachings of the Dharma can certainly serve as ethical precepts for children. Non-violence and not harming any living thing, for example, can be easily understood by a child. But most importantly we teach children about mindfulness, compassion and awareness through example. You cannot make children want to be spiritual and they may well reject everything you teach them as they form their own opinions. They have their own karma and must follow their own journey which may or may not be to our liking. But, hopefully, the example they see in their parents will sow the seeds for flowers of Dharma that will awaken when the time is right.

At the core of all religions lie the same basic human values: truth, right conduct, peace, compassion and non-violence. For example, perhaps you may want to show your children that we need only to look at what is happening in our own society, and in the world generally, to know what is *wrong* conduct. What do the advertisements and media show them about human values? Dharma embraces so many more aspects than can be translated by any one word or phrase: duty, righteousness, good conduct, consideration for others each covers only part of the meaning. Let your children know when you see the Dharma manifesting in human kindness or when it expresses itself as selfless service. In addition, you may enhance your children's knowledge of the core values of Dharma by means of stories, quotations, prayers and music and song. Discuss human values with them and encourage them to look into their own hearts to find the truth, perhaps suggesting that they sit for a few moments in silence in order to 'hear' more clearly what their heart tells them.

Application

The love of infinite mothers

Central to Hinduism is the protecting Mother-Goddesses (*Matrikas* or *Matris*). They are said to appear in repulsive guise, as does the great Mother-Goddess Kali; for so beautiful are they in their true form that if seen directly by the unperfected *yogin* they would be apt to arouse in him uncontrollable sensual desire. As you now know, Tibetan wisdom drew much of its inspiration from India and integrated both Hindu and Buddhist wisdom and beliefs. The synthesis of ideas found in Tibetan teachings brings us close to the essence of Eastern wisdom. And the mother, as a symbol, is central to these ideas.

The *Ma-nam-mkhah-ma* prayer refers to mothers as being infinite in number as the heavens are in expanse. Tibetan Buddhism, of course, believes in reincarnation and that over many lives we take both male and female incarnations. Every sentient being has therefore, at some time in the course of innumerable cycles of rebirth, experienced the self-sacrificing love of being a mother. How right it is that maternity units now allow both parents to be present at the birth of their child. The motherly love learnt from past lives can be awakened in unison. In addition, the child that is about to be born may have shared past lives with you before and this precious moment of reunion should not be missed.

A technique we can use ourselves draws upon one of the most ancient meditation techniques of the Tibetan monks.

1. Make yourself comfortable. Sit on the floor or on a straight-backed chair. Place your hands in the gesture of meditation as you did in Chapter 3. Bend your neck down slightly and let your tongue touch the roof of your mouth near the top of your teeth. Relax. Close your eyes and be aware of how your breathing is slowing down and your mind is becoming still.
2. As you sink deeper into meditation imagine the love of the millions of mothers that suckled you in your past lives. Feel how much they loved you as their precious baby. Sense that warm universal love that is inherent deep within every

sentient being. Know how you, no matter what your sex now, were also once a mother. Extend that maternal love to touch the soul of every living thing. As you become more absorbed in these feelings you may marvel at how every human being and life form has experienced these feelings. Recognise the universality of motherly love. See it like a warm pink light that enfolds the universe filling every part, every atom with warm loving light.

3 Know that love and compassion fill the universe.

4 Now imagine that you are a million mothers giving their love to a million babies. Feel how your love soothes and brings joy. Now see how the love flows back to you. Extend this feeling to all sentient beings. Every animal, plant, human being was once in the infinity of time your mother or your baby. Extend motherly love to all and absorb motherly love from all.

5 Meditate in this way and you will touch the source of the loving fellowship that bonds all life together. You can adapt this technique into your day to day life as well. See in every person you meet a loving mother. Feel the warmth that is deep inside them and extend your own paternal warmth to them also. By doing this you unite your soul with theirs on a subtle, transcendental level.

Chapter 6
What can the timeless wisdom of Tibet teach us about marriage, the home and our friends?

When Buddhism began to spread throughout India, Shakyamuni Buddha was accused of introducing a spiritual method by which families were left without sons, women were widowed and the line of succession of a clan was cut off. At the same time, the recluses were saying that it is impossible to seek salvation in the restrictive conditions of a household and so sought out the homeless life. There was a great deal of controversy in the air as Buddhism became a major influence upon Indian society.

But Shakyamuni Buddha's teachings were not aimed only at the recluses, although this tradition had existed for many centuries prior to Shakyamuni Buddha's time. However, the early scriptures say that it is also possible for the lay householder to attain the goal of the Buddhist way and many ordinary people attained nirvana despite not following the homeless life of an *Arahant*.

As Buddhism and Tibetan Buddhism comes West there is a danger that some of its ideas may become watered down as they are taken up by Westerners. Our society's objectives are getting, becoming, having and retaining whereas the path to liberation advises the opposite: letting go, not becoming, just being and renunciation. Honest Buddhist practice requires an inner revolution and not just the improvement of one's ethics and behaviour. Dharma is pure, it cannot be diluted.

It is important, however, that the lay practitioner lives according to the precepts taught by Shakyamuni Buddha. As it says in the *Dighanikaya*

Morality is washed all round with wisdom, and wherever there is wisdom there is morality. From the observing of the moralities comes wisdom and from the observing of wisdom comes morality. Morality and wisdom together reveal the height of the world. It is just as if one should wash one hand with the other or one foot with the other; exactly so is morality washed round with wisdom and wisdom with morality."

These principles can be applied equally to the homeless or householder's life.

Shakyamuni Buddha gave guidance of how the layperson should best employ this philosophy in everyday life. Regarding the relationship between husband and wife he said that there are five ways in which a husband should minister to his wife. He must 'be courteous to her, not despise her, be faithful to her, hand over authority to her and provide her with necessary adornments. In return, the wife should minister to her husband: by ordering the household well, by hospitality to their relatives, by fidelity, by taking care of his wealth, and by her industry.'

Shakyamuni Buddha also spoke of other important issues and in the *Anguttara Nikaya* advises girls who are about to marry to 'rise early, work willingly, order their affairs smoothly and cultivate gentle voices.' Shakyamuni Buddha also recognised the difficulties that their gender faced and, in particular, the problems that occurred in those times when they were called upon to leave their own family and live with their husband's family.

In essence we, our loved ones, our friends and all beings are the embodiment of wisdom and compassion as represented in the image of Shakyamuni Buddha. Becoming aware of this gives us an important understanding. If we are all One then why do we have desire and attachment which gives rise to clinging, delusion and hatred. It is our duty to help all people. But we continue to make distinctions: we say 'I' 'you', 'my partner' and 'my friend', etc. This brings with it expectations and the negative results that come with them. However, if we can be free of expectation and judgement then we are not bound by this negativity.

Tibetan Buddhism places a lot of emphasis upon the need to always consider the welfare of others. In the *Bodhicaryavatara* there is an explanation of meditation techniques for cultivating *Bodhicitta*, the aspiration to achieve enlightenment for the benefit of all living beings. The key is to recognise that just as I want to find happiness and freedom from suffering so, too, all other living beings wish for the same. Just as we work hard to achieve our own liberation so, too, we must work just as hard for the benefit of others. They are as inseparable from ourselves as are our arms, legs, head, etc. from our body. Another's suffering is our own. Therefore, we should not discriminate between ourselves and others in working to gain happiness and overcome suffering.

It is also important to remember that just as we have a natural right to be happy so, too, all beings have this same birthright. The welfare of others must encompass the infinite number of beings that fill existence. Personal happiness cannot be achieved without renouncing selfishness. From a practical standpoint it is clear to see that the more we work for the benefit of others the more benefit we achieve ourselves. Selfish and self-centred individuals remain lonely and miserable whereas the person who is generous of spirit will always attract good things into their life. Also, recognising the Buddhahood that resides within other sentient beings brings us closer to recognising the same within ourselves.

Shakyamuni Buddha made it clear that the quality of making friends is important. In the text *Dighanikaya* he says

> *The person who is kindly, who makes friends, makes welcome, is free from avarice, is understanding, is a conciliator, such a one obtains good repute. Generosity, kindly speech, doing good to whatever person, fairness in all things, everywhere, as is fit and proper, these are indeed the means on which the world turns, just as a chariot moves on quickly depending on the pin of a wheel axle.*

By reducing the tenacity of our self-centred attitudes and increasing our concern for others we naturally become much more happy. By helping in this way we attract friends quite naturally and share a common happiness. Most of our worries and misery is caused by self-centredness, but when you do service to others all these problems evaporate. This same rule applies even in people who have no spiritual motive in their work. The positive state of mind will attract people who may be ready to offer assistance.

No matter how spiritual a person, it is natural that they have close friends who care and show concern. It is good to share our joys with others and lighten the world with our smiles. We should delight in our sincere friendships.

A warm-hearted person is closer to the heart of Shakyamuni Buddha's teachings than someone who scowls at the world and harbours resentment. Happiness and good humour are clear signs of spiritual progress. Consciously trying to benefit others, directly or indirectly, is what makes life meaningful.

The Tibetan Buddhist will reflect deeply about the advantages of concern for others' welfare and the disadvantages of self-centredness. By trusting the message of Shakyamuni Buddha and seeing the Buddha in everyone, they learn to be tolerant and considerate. The enlightened being shows the same concern towards all beings that a mother shows her only child. Tibetan Buddhists extend their compassion to everybody – even to those who would be their enemy. Their greatest goal is to work effortlessly and spontaneously for others and, on this basis, take refuge in the Buddhas and bodhisattvas.

In his book *Awakening the Mind, Lightening the Heart,* the Dalai Lama summarises these simple ideas with his usual succinct flourish:

> *If you manage not to tell lies, to be honest, to praise the Buddhas and bodhisattvas and to inspire others to work toward the achievement of Buddhahood, then naturally the four corresponding negative activities will cease. (Lies, hypocrisy, delusion and discouragement.) I do not think this is too difficult if you try. In short, be a kind, warm-hearted*

person, and for the rest of your life try to help other people. If you are unable to help them, at least refrain from harming them. If you lead an honest and meaningful life now, the future will take care of itself.

> ### Illustration
>
> ### Service to others
>
> One morning, when Shakyamuni Buddha was on his way to the house of Anathapindika he heard a loud commotion being caused by a woman named Sujata. She had been brought from a wealthy family and was rebelling against her parents-in-law or her husband. She was also disrespectful of the Buddha. Shakyamuni Buddha asked Anathapindika to bring Sujata to him. As she sat by his side he explained that there were seven kinds of wives: one like an executioner inflicting punishment, one like a thief, one like a mistress, one like a mother, one like a sister, one like a companion, and one like a slave. 'Which of the seven are you Sujata?' inquired Shakyamuni Buddha.
>
> Sujata replied that his categories were so succinct that it was impossible to answer unless he explained himself in more detail. Shakyamuni Buddha continued telling her that the executioner wife was pitiless and corrupt like a prostitute, the thief robbed her husband of his wealth and the mistress spoke only lazy gossip. However, the mother-wife cared for her husband and his possessions like a child, the sister-wife behaved like a younger sister to an elder and the companion-wife behaved like a companion. The slave-wife endured all things. She would remain calm and pure in heart and obedient.
>
> 'Which of the seven are you?' repeated Shakyamuni Buddha
>
> Sujata said that she would be the seventh kind. Shakyamuni Buddha explained that the last four kinds of wife would, at death, enter a heavenly world.

Many of the problems we encounter in life are caused because we refuse to accept life as it is. We feel that we have to change the world around us and, in particular, we try to change the people we love. Most husbands and wives spend a great deal of time trying to mould their partner into someone they'd like them to be. Then they complain saying 'You're not the person I married!' We must all respect each other's individuality and realise that, like the world itself, we cannot possess anything. It is not for us to change other people, it is our duty to change ourselves and be a good example. The world and the people around us are like sand that slips through our fingers. Transience is the nature of all things. The truth is that we cannot grasp anything, even the mind. To believe otherwise is an illusion.

A spiritually healthy way to learn this lesson of transience and acceptance is to observe the nature of our own mind. Once we realise the nature of ourselves we may become aware of how the same rules apply to all things. When we cease to grasp after the things of the world and cease to try to possess we gain a simple happiness that is not dependent on anything or anyone. We become free and will then be able to give our love to the world in a spirit of service.

Application

Mahamudra

Mahamudra is basically sitting down, letting the mind relax, standing back and looking at the coming and going of thoughts. It is extremely simple to do yet is, perhaps, the greatest meditation technique of all.

1 Make yourself comfortable. Sit on the floor or on a straight-backed chair. Place your hands in the gesture of meditation as you did in Chapter 3. Bend your neck down slightly and let your tongue touch the roof of your mouth near the top of your teeth. Relax. Close your eyes and be aware of how your breathing is slowing down and your mind is becoming still.

2 Allow yourself to become deeply relaxed yet simultaneously maintain a keen alertness and awareness.
3 Be aware of the coming and going of your thoughts. Do not try to produce or impede them. Don't get interested in them, instead just watch them like waves rising and falling on the ocean surface.
4 Notice how thoughts by their nature are quite transparent. As you watch the thoughts in this way you will observe how they spontaneously slow down as the mind becomes more and more relaxed.
5 Once the thoughts become slower watch for the gaps between thought. Your true awareness has a pristine clarity. In these spaces between thought lies the true mind. It is like the clear blue sky that you see when the clouds move away.
6 Mahamudra is often done at the end of the main visualisation practice. Then you allow the mind just to relax into its innate emptiness. In this clear void of awareness between the thoughts is the emptiness of mind.
7 Ask yourself if awareness, the thought and the stillness behind the thought are the same. Or are they different? You may want to question what's happening to you in order to understand your own direct experience.

Chapter 7
What can the timeless wisdom of Tibet teach us about work and money?

The great Tibetan poet Milarepa, said: 'All worldly pursuits have but the one unavoidable and inevitable end, which is sorrow: acquisitions end in dispersion; buildings, in destruction; meetings, in separation; births, in death.' His words are so similar to the words in the Bible that say 'I have seen all the works that are done under the sun; and behold, all is vanity and vexation of spirit.' (Ecclesiastes 1.14.)

According to Tibetan Buddhism, we should put an end to the 'Eight Worldly Ambitions' which are: Profit, and Avoidance of Loss; Fame, and Avoidance of Defamation; Praise, and Avoidance of Disparagement; Pleasure, and Avoidance of Pain. Instead the yogin should strive towards the 'Four Boundless Wishes'.

These qualities must so fill the nature of the yogin as to radiate from him, as divine compassion. This includes people and, if they are using Tantric magic, also towards all the unenlightened genii, demons and elementals. For the Tibetan, release from material desires helps the adept on the path to enlightenment and even has the additional benefit of bestowing protective magical powers. In time, even these benefits must be surrendered for the sake of all sentient beings.

Although most of us are not engaged in the pursuit of magic, our goal is nonetheless the same as the lonely Tibetan recluse. We, too, seek enlightenment but in our lives we cannot easily turn our back on the world and seek the solitude of the monk's cell or the cave. We must live in the midst of samsara yet still, somehow, overcome the material demons that want to draw us back into ignorance. Today, the threats do not come as black headed demons surrounded by wheels of fire but in a far more deadly form. Modern advertising psychology tries to seduce us into greater and greater materialism.

I've sat in boardrooms and marketing think tanks aimed at finding the right combination of words and imagery that will seduce the target audience to buy the desired product. The methods draw on propaganda techniques and psychology and are applied with the strategy a military campaign. These are today's unenlightened genii, demons and elementals that we have to overcome except they're far more subtle and disguised as glossy products. In my opinion there's nothing wrong with a consumer society but there's a terrible malady in the greed motives that fuel it. It's good to have comfort but must we have luxury? It's good to have respect but must we have status? It's good to have control but must we have power? And it's good to have security but do we need to hide from reality?

The result of our materialism is that we are becoming a society of spiritual weaklings. The more that you grasp after the material the greater becomes your inner loneliness, your fear of death and your insecurity. The material world offers no solace, there is nothing in it that will support you or give you refuge. Everything is subject to decay. It is all transient, even your precious body that you pamper. And this is what Shakyamuni Buddha realised was an eternal truth that applies to every age.

Shakyamuni Buddha knew, as all Enlightened Ones know, that happiness and joy are the normal state of human true nature but they have fallen into an illusionary trap that brings much suffering. We presume that the causes of our unhappiness, frustration and suffering lie in the things around us such as the blows of fate, the hostility of other people, bad luck, etc. But Shakyamuni Buddha realised that the source of these troubles lies within ourselves and is rooted in our desires, leading to craving for, and clinging to, the transient things of the material world. This selfish desire is driven by the twin forces of delusion and ignorance of things as they really are.

We martyr ourselves because of our egoism, envy and greed– the three pillars of the advertising industry– and deny ourselves the inherent joy that is the true nature of our inner consciousness. When we examine our lives, and perhaps meditate upon those things that we desire, it becomes self-evident that it is our desire that causes us such pain and disappointment.

Fortunately, Shakyamuni Buddha found a cure for our illness which he prescribed in the form of the Noble Eightfold Path of Right View, Right Resolve, Right Speech, Right Conduct, Right Livelihood, Right Effort, Right Awareness and Right Contemplation. The essence of his cure is to is to steer a path between the two extremes of sensual indulgence on the one hand and harsh austerities on the other. To understand how to apply his teachings to our work and money we need to consider his fifth path: Right Livelihood.

Right Livelihood is closely related to the fourth path, Right Conduct, which tells us that all action must be correct according to a high ethical and moral code. This means that we must cause no harm to anyone and, as far as possible, avoid injury to any kind of life. In addition, it means that we should allow compassion for all sentient beings to be our driving force and at the same time remove all negative emotions such as anger, lust greed, etc. Our livelihood must, therefore, also follow these principles and our daily work should bring some good to humankind. It may be difficult in today's world to find a livelihood that directly benefits anyone except a corporation but, at the very least, we should endeavour to find something that does not directly bring harm to others.

We must, therefore, examine our conscience. Does your livelihood bring harm to humanity either directly or indirectly? You may not necessarily work for an armaments factory or an abattoir but I expect there are many aspects about your job that may prick your conscience. Inevitably you will have to make some compromises, but if your job does real harm to others then you would be advised to seriously consider making some changes and perhaps find some other means of livelihood.

The karmic effects of what you do may also bring you harm. For example, I recently took out a Life Assurance policy with a company that will invest only in companies that have green credentials. If I had chosen another route such as signing with a company that invested in armaments or the tobacco industry then I'd be generating negative karma by my actions and I'd therefore be more likely to die sooner! Spiritually and materially I'd be the loser.

Shakyamuni Buddha named specific trades that a Buddhist should not do. Traditionally the layperson is barred from dealing in arms, in living beings, in flesh, in intoxicating drinks and in poison. In addition, to practise deceit, treachery, soothsaying, trickery, prostitution and usury is regarded as wrong living. The layperson should also be free from acquisitiveness or any connections with money making, legal or otherwise. The homeless life is the ideal path without family and business responsibilities and with nearly all one's time devoted to meditation.

Sadly, soothsaying is included in the trades to avoid and is another reason I am not a practising Buddhist. My own livelihood as a medium, psychic and author inevitably involves this, but I know they can be of great benefit to others. However, I'm not alone as Tibetan Buddhism employs a great number of divinitory techniques. Perhaps the answer is that we should always look deeply into what we do and examine the motive behind our actions. If compassion is the motivating force then ethically we won't go far wrong.

Avoidance of a negative livelihood and its resultant negative karma is important but not the end of the story. We must also use our livelihood to actively help humanity. This doesn't mean to say that we should all become charity workers but we can nonetheless transform our work into a holy act. We should see everything we do as being for the benefit of all sentient beings and, therefore, give up the fruits of our work. In other words, we should not strive for the result but transform the work itself into our spiritual practice. In this way we acquire divine wealth.

If, instead of pursuing the transitory values of this world, we keep our sights on expanding our compassion and dedicate our work to the One, then inevitably the karmic forces that unfold in our life will bring us to the ultimate goal of compassion which is enlightenment. This cannot fail. Compassion is the hub of the eight-spoke wheel.

Unfortunately, everyone today is seeking comfort and pleasure as if it is the be-all and end-all. We are like gluttonous children in a sweet shop who have been told we can eat anything and everything we like but have not been warned that this overindulgence will make us sick and, perhaps, even seriously ill. It is our duty to our own welfare to develop self-control, good habits, good attitudes, good behaviour and good character. Without these we are traitors to ourselves.

Illustration

Vigilance

Shakyamuni Buddha gave a great deal of practical advice about livelihood and how to best work for the good of all. King Pasenadi once asked him if there were anything of profit attainable in the things of the present which would also be of value in the world beyond. Shakyamuni Buddha's reply was simple: 'Vigilance'. Again this illustrated that its not the material that's important but the human motivation that's behind it.

Shakyamuni Buddha also said that there are five reasons that a person should desire to possess means:
1 By hard work to make parents, partner, children and employees happy.
2 To make friends and companions happy.
3 To prevent property from harm from fire, water, rulers, robbers, enemies and heirs.
4 To make suitable offerings to kin, guests, deceased, kings and devas.

5 To be able to institute, over time, offerings to recluses engaged in the perfecting of themselves.

Wealth is therefore gained in an honourable way in order to benefit others. It should be circulated rather than accumulated. Shakyamuni Buddha also said that miserly behaviour was a wasteful and bad way to utilise wealth. A wealthy person should allocate wealth properly in order to be happier and also make others happy. Charitable deeds and almsgiving are productive of a happy future state.

Shakyamuni Buddha also advised that one's income, excluding alms which is by discretion, should be divided into four parts. One quarter should be used by the householder for his or her own ease and convenience, a half should be used for the householder's business or occupation and the remaining quarter should be saved in case of adversity. Wise counsel, I believe, which I use as the golden rule when planning my business income. The quarter put away is usually used for the dreaded taxcollector.

Application

How selfish and materialistic are you?

It is hard to see ourselves as others see us and even more difficult to see ourselves as we really are. How selfish and materialistic are you? The truth may come as a shock. In the classic Buddhist text *A Guide to the Bodhisattva's Way of Life* is a meditation technique designed to help you confront hardships and transform them into more positive conditions. The following exercise may help you see yourself as you really are and make a few changes for the better.

1 Make yourself comfortable. Sit on the floor or on a straight-backed chair. Place your hands in the gesture of meditation as you did in Chapter 3. Bend your neck down slightly and let your tongue touch the roof of your mouth near the top of your teeth. Relax. Close your eyes and be aware of how your breathing is slowing down and your mind is becoming still.

2 Allow yourself to become deeply relaxed yet simultaneously maintain a keen alertness and awareness.

3 Now imagine that you can see yourself. You can see your face and your body but you can also see into the very essence of your present nature. See yourself at your most egotistical. You are the embodiment of self-centredness and materialistic selfishness.

4 Now imagine that the 'you' that you see is standing in front of a group of people. These are a cross-section of people and represent all the millions of sentient beings that fill the universe. Keep the pictures in your mind, moving from the group to 'you' then back to the group, and so on.

5 Next, you must adopt a third person's point of view which is as the neutral, unbiased observer. Now make a comparative assessment of the value, the interests and the importance of these two groups. Ask yourself what faults you have, particularly those that are oblivious of the well-being of other sentient beings. What does your selfishness achieve?

6 Turn your attention to the group of people. What are their needs? How do they suffer? How can you help them? Whose needs are the greater?

7 From the neutral, unattached viewpoint you will soon see that the interests and well-being of others are more important. As your compassion for the group continues and your selfish attachments decrease, you will feel more compassion towards the infinite other sentient beings that this small crowd represents. Feel how the more your compassion grows the greater becomes your inner strength. See how compassion for the welfare of others releases you from the need for selfish gain and rushing after your own self-interests.

Chapter 8
What can the timeless wisdom of Tibet teach us about health?

Tibet developed its own form of yoga based upon a synthesis of Indian Hatha yoga and the Chinese systems. The benefits of yoga are well known: it brings health, vitality and alertness and is said to keep away all disease and illness. The Tibetan system uses similar yoga postures, practises breathing exercises and makes use of the chakras which are vortexes of energy which unite the spiritual and physical bodies. Tibetan yoga also uses the latent Kundalini energy centred at the base of the spine and raises its energy through the chakras. This awakens the Siddhi energies and triggers the practitioner's psychic powers.

The objective of all yoga paths is to dissipate Ignorance and to guide the yogin to what the Buddhists call Right Knowledge. It requires discipline of body and mind. As the *Udanavarga* of the Tibetan canonical scriptures tells us, 'Whoever hath lived in accordance with this law of discipline, in gentleness and purity, will, having transcended deaths and births, put an end to his sorrow.' The Hindu, Patanjali, explains that when the mind and body are brought under control and freed from passion then spiritual insight arises together with knowledge of previous incarnations. Yoga enables humans to transcend the human state and see beyond the illusionary sense perceptions and objects of the phenomenal world. And, of course, it dispels the illusion of the self as a thing separate from all other selves.

A master of yoga has complete control over his or her body. The master can make the body immune to each of the elements and even to gravitation. Using these techniques, the Tibetan yogis such as Milarepa were able to perform incredible paranormal and physical feats. Western travellers returning from Tibet prior to the Chinese occupation told stories of men who could sit naked in the freezing winds and use their yogic powers to melt the snow around them. (This practice is known as the *Tumo* initiation.) Also, there are tales of how some lamas survive for years at a time without food, run at incredible speeds, are sealed into caves, climb mountains as if they are flying and send telepathic messages on the wind (*dubchens*)

These practices that combine mental concentration and various breathing gymnastics come under the collective Tibetan term *lung-gom*. The effects ascribed to lung-gom training vary considerably but is especially used for a kind of training which is to develop amazing nimbleness. In particular, this enables its adepts to take incredibly long walks at an amazing speed. The lung-gom-pas who practised these techniques were revered throughout Tibet. If one was seen travelling at great speed across the landscape nobody would stop him or speak to him for fear of breaking his concentration for this would most certainly kill the practitioner. Lama long-gom-pas were said to draw upon the power of a god who they control by repetition of a *ngags* (like a mantra). If the trance-like meditation is broken and the god's spirit leaves prematurely then the lama long-gom-pa dies instantly. Training for these miraculous feats usually takes place at night. Some initiates of the secret lore say that the feet of the lung-gom-pa never touch the ground and that they glide in the air. There are stories of long-gom-pas who would wear chains to stop them floating away like a balloon!

We may never know how many of these tales are true, although from what I've see in India I have no reason to doubt it. Tibetan yoga certainly has much to offer the West and there are now many organisations outside Tibet that teach their yoga techniques. Extraordinary powers may serve as an illustration of what can be achieved by using these methods but is by no means the goal of most practitioners. The main benefits are good health, posture and vitality which will benefit meditation.

Tibetan medicine

Perhaps one of the greatest healing legacies that Tibet has left humankind, and which the West is only just beginning to discover, is its medicine which has been practised for over 2,500 years. It is still taught by the Tibetans in exile and has even been accepted by the Chinese invaders. Although it hovered near extinction for 40 years since the destruction of the main medical school opposite the Poala Palace, it is now thriving even under the Chinese occupation. There is now a newly enlarged 1,000-bed hospital in Lhasa which practices only Tibetan medicine and a factory that produces medicine in the traditional way with prayers and the use of astrology.

The headquarters of the *Tibetan Medical and Astrological Institute* are now based in Dharamsala in Northern India. Here, many new Tibetan doctors are being trained and the ancient medicines are again being manufactured. Today, there are over 30 branches in India and Nepal and many new practitioners in Europe and America. For hundreds of years it has been known about in Russia and extensive experiments were carried out in the Buryat Scientific Centre of the Siberian Branch of the Russian Academy of Sciences. Many of the Tibetan plants can be substituted, they discovered, by Mongolian varieties. Fortunately, because of the vigorous efforts of its doctors, a large portion of Tibetan medicine is being preserved.

There is a tremendous amount that Western medicine can learn from Tibetan pharmacology that utilised the rare plants and herbs found only in Tibet. Dieticians, too, can learn a great deal from the simple remedies that say, for example, that pomegranates can cure indigestion to the carefully constructed diets designed to cure specific illnesses. We may take time to assimilate curative practices such as blood letting, astrology, moxibustion, cupping, mineral baths or cold showers but should respect the tradition that these beliefs came from. For example, the *Four Pharmacopoeias* is an epoch-making text written 1,100 years ago and anticipates many of the findings of modern medicine. It even understood the way a human embryo grows within the womb and distinguishes 'the fish stage' (corresponding to the aquatic creature), 'the tortoise stage' (corresponding to the reptile) and 'the pig stage' (corresponding to the mammal). Also, whilst it may not offer modern Western medicine much in areas of infectious diseases or surgery, it is in chronic afflictions, psychosomatic and psychological imbalance that its application appears to offer the greatest possibilities.

Tibetan medicine is one of the five major sciences and is called *gSoba Rig-pa*, the science of healing. It is much more than herbalism although it uses various herbs and trees, rocks, resins, soils, saps and precious metals. (There are more than 1,000 medicinal herbs, 144 minerals and 150 types of raw materials of animal origin in the normal Tibetan medicine cabinet.) These are used to make seven kinds of precious pill known as *Rinchen rilpo* which are given after the physician has made a lengthy diagnosis. Tibetan medicine is good for all kinds of illness but is claimed to be particularly successful in its treatment of chronic diseases such as rheumatism, arthritis, ulcers, chronic digestive problems, asthma, hepatitis, eczema, liver problems, sinus problems, anxiety and troubles with the nervous system.

Tibetan medicine takes an approach to diagnosis and cure completely different from Western medicine. The Tibetan physician looks upon the human organism as one unit and uses healing techniques to re-establish balance throughout the whole organism. The initial examination of the patient is a long procedure. First, the doctor and patient drink tea together and talk about themselves. In particular, the doctor wants to know about the patient's occupation, emotional problems and dreams. Only after this will the physician begin the physical examination. This, too, may seem strange to Westerners. The doctor will begin smelling the patient's skin and observing its colour, and may need to feel parts of the body and then take the patient's pulse. Tibetan doctors distinguish about 300 kinds of pulse from which they can ascertain the state of all the internal organs. From it, they can also make judgements about current and future diseases and about longevity. The doctor will use both hands to examine the pulse. The left wrist of the male patient is read first and the right wrist is read first for the female patient.

The next step is to examine the patient's urine that would have been taken first thing in the morning prior to the appointment. Again, smell is important and the doctor will also note the way the bubbles form when it is whisked with a chopstick. If it is still and white, the person has a cold nature and the circulation will be slow. For this, the doctor may prescribe warm potency herbs. Big bubbles in the urine indicate food poisoning.

Diet is also an extremely important part of Tibetan remedies and contradicts some of our Western notions. For example, fat is only a problem for people whose digestive fires are not stoked. To avoid heart attacks cooked meats with warming spices are recommended. Sweets are also considered good and will help with coughs and problems with the eyes. Also, simple common sense with eating is important. It is stressed particularly that it is important to eat in the evening before 8 p.m. so food can be digested by 10 p.m.

Tibetan medicine also takes spiritual considerations into account and believes that every person is subordinate to cosmic laws. In particular, medical astrology is used when making a diagnosis which is claimed also to predict possible diseases in the future. The cosmic conditions influence the amount of healing energy called *tsi* or *prana* that a person is absorbing. This comes to the person from the environment, the air the person breathes and from food. It then passes along the body's energy lines, called the meridians, and circulates throughout the body giving life and energy. A dramatic loss of tsi is considered to be one of the major causes of disease. In addition, the Tibetans believe that mental and emotional states, such as desire and anger, can have a damaging effect on health. A Tibetan doctor is just as likely to prescribe meditation and eating at the correct time as a pill or herbal remedy.

The Tibetans believe that there are long-term and short-term causes of disease and that the ultimate cause of all is ignorance of reality. Clinging to personal self gives rise to three mental poisons that pollute the body: desires, hatred and stupidity. Together these are the long-term causes of illness. Short-term causes of illness are known as the three humours: *rLung* (wind energy), *mKhris-pa* (bile energy) and *Bad-kan* (phlegm). These are produced by the three mental poisons. Desires give rise to wind, hatred to bile and stupidity to phlegm. The Tibetan doctor decides what humours are out of balance before he offers a treatment. There follows a brief explanation of the three humours with some traditional common-sense remedies that don't involve drugs or surgery. For a complete diagnosis and treatment you would, of course, need to visit a qualified Tibetan doctor.

The three humours

rLung (wind energy)

This is a subtle flow of energy that is both cold and hot. It mainly controls breathing and the movements of mind, speech and body. It is symbolised by a bird and its element is air. It is described as rough, light, cool, thin, hard and movable. rLung energy helps with growth, movement of the body, breathing and the functions of the mind and speech. It also aides digestion by separating in our stomach what we eat into nutrients and waste products.

The rLung type: Excess rLung makes the person thoughtful, active and restless. The person will also be sexually active and sprone to psychological illness. Insomnia, anxiety, asthma and heart conditions linked to stress and back pains are connected with rLung. These types are thin and sweat little. They have a bad memory and lack concentration. Desire is the cause of their anxieties and tension.

Remedies: The cure is deep relaxation and a little meditation, but not in the extreme and definitely no fasting. If you have excess rLung, you should avoid too much sex and get plenty of sleep. Idle chatter and tension should be avoided. Dark or warm places are good for you, as is beautiful scenery. Try not to worry and surround yourself with friends and loved ones. rLung problems can be caused by eating too many light foods such as pork, goat's meat, milk and yoghurt, strong tea or coffee, soya, vegetables, pulses, skimmed milk. According to the Tibetans an excess of these foods which we in the West consider healthy can, in reality, create a bodily imbalance. It is advised that you eat food which is heavy and has a high nutritional potency such as lamb, butter, molasses, alcohol, milk, soups, chicken, garlic, ginger and onions. Herbal cures include: aqullaria agollocha, allium sativum, myristica fragrans, asafoetida and santalum album.

mKhris-pa (bile energy)

This humour is hot like fire and controls heat in the body. It is symbolised by the snake and is especially linked to the liver and digestion. Its nature is hot and has the qualities of being oily, sharp, light, pungent and moist. As well as body temperature it also helps with the digestion of food and is what causes us to feel hungry or thirsty at the right times. It keeps the skin's pores clear.

The mKhris-pa type: The mKhris-pa types are angry and impatient but also ambitious, cleaver and quick witted. They are susceptible to physical illnesses such as eczema, sinus, headaches, nausea and diseases of the liver may cause problems. The mKhris-pa person is likely to be of medium build, sweat a lot and have an analytical mind. Anger and hatred are their weaknesses which causes overheating and gall-bladder problems.

Remedies: The mKhris-pa person needs cooling things such as salads and cold drinks. Light physical exercise such as walking or yoga is of benefit as are visualisation exercises to quieten the mind. If you have excess mKhris-pa, cold baths and showers and walks by the sea will re-balance you. Use a cool perfume such as sandalwood. Alcohol and spiced foods are harmful to you. mKhris-pa problems are caused by eating an excess of: milk, alcohol, meat, full-fat cheese, nuts, sugar, ice cream, lard, butter and chocolates. You should avoid heavy exercise and definitely don't go jogging or do any exercise that involves jerking the body. It is suggested that you eat beef, vegetables, fresh butter, fresh low fat cheese, cow's yoghurt, weak tea, spring water and eat less greasy food. Herbal cures include: swertia chirata, momordica charantia, holarrhena antidysenterica, aconitum naviculare, ixers gracilis, chrysosplenium nepalense, swertia hookeri and berberis asiatica.

Bad-kan (phlegm energy)

Symbolised by the pig, this humour is cold like water or the moon and controls bodily fluids and the immune system. It is related to water and earth and is connected with all illnesses that are cold in nature. It is described as oily, cool, heavy, blunt, smooth, steady and sticky. Bad-kan sustains the bodily fluids and it helps to keep the joints flexible.

The Bad-kan type: These people are stable and patient but susceptible to chronic problems of the sinus and digestive system. Asthma, bronchial and kidney problems are likely. Physically, they are often fat. Also they are slow with their movements and have a tendency to laziness. They hate arguments and will avoid confrontation. They eat the wrong foods and are easily misguided.

Remedies: Warm food and strenuous exercise. If you have excess Bad-kan, inactivity can cause Bad-kan problems so make sure you do lots of exercise such as walking or running. A holiday in the sun or sitting by a warm fire will help restore your balance. Too much raw food can cause can cause an imbalance in Bad-kan. Avoid uncooked meat, salad, raw fish, cold drinks and raw milk. Do not sleep during the day or after heavy meals. Cold showers, too-light clothing or working where it's damp are also to be avoided. The foods you should eat include: honey, mutton, fish, barley, wine, ginger, cooked vegetables and drink plenty of hot water. Herbal cures include: chaenomeles, inula helenium, coriandium sativum, meconopis discigera, punica granatum, kaempferia galanga and phyllantus emblica.

When all three humours (*Nyipa sum*) are in balance then what the Tibetans call the seven bodily sustainers[1] are also in balance and the person will experience good health. It is much more likely for a Tibetan doctor to prescribe meditation, a change in lifestyle or diet before resorting to surgery.

---

[1] The seven sustainers are: essential nutrients, blood, muscle tissues, fat, bone, marrow and regenerative fluid (sperm or ovum).

Illustration

The cause of illness

The Tibetans knew a great deal about the human anatomy because of their practice of 'Sky Burial' in which a corpse was cut into pieces and fed on a mountain top to carrion birds. (This was a practical method because Tibet has so little arable land.) Despite their knowledge, Tibetan doctors believe that it is far better to cure the organ than to remove it. Surgery is considered as a violent way of curing a condition.

It is far better to treat the cause of the illness. For example, a weed will continue to grow no matter how often we cut away its leaves. But if we remove its root then the weed will die. So too with the illness. Sometimes, a quick solution is not possible, the cause may be from many previous lifetimes of negative karma. But when a person employs the methods of Tibetan medicine and also calls upon the powers of the mantras[2] dedicated to the Medicine Buddha (*Bhaisajya-guru* or *Menlha* in Tibetan) then not only the illness but the root of the illness will be eradicated. The patient will not only be free of the condition in this life but in his next incarnation as well. Shakyamuni Buddha is recorded as saying that by uttering the Bhaisajya-guru mantra, one is free of the nine untimely causes of death and of all suffering. All subsequent reincarnations will be 'peaceful and joyous' (Birnbaum, *Snow Lion*, p88)

Application

The healing light of tsi energy

The cause of many of the diseases affecting modern people is that we have forgotten how to extract tsi from the things around us. You will remember that this is the living energy also known as prana that constitutes our aura and flows through the meridians and chakras of the body. It is the life

---

[2] The mantras used during the preparation of herbs and pills are usually taken from works such as *The Medicine Guru Beams of Lapis Lazuli Sutra* and *Four Secret Oral Tantras on the Eight Branches of the Essence of Nectar*.

force. Tsi can be drawn from our food and from water but also from nature. High levels of tsi may be found near waterfalls, high in the mountains or in sacred places where the earth exudes this energy. It is also in the air we breathe and for our next exercise we will use a simple technique to draw tsi energy into ourselves.

1 Make yourself comfortable. Sit on the floor or on a straight-backed chair. Place your hands in the gesture of meditation as you did in Chapter 3. Bend your neck down slightly and let your tongue touch the roof of your mouth near the top of your teeth. Relax. Close your eyes and be aware of how your breathing is slowing down and your mind is becoming still.

2 Allow yourself to become deeply relaxed yet simultaneously maintain a keen alertness and awareness.

3 Now visualise that in the space in front of you is the Medicine Buddha. He is surrounded by a deep blue light, the colour of the sacred stone Lapis Lazuli. He is smiling serenely and you see how he is sitting on a lotus with a moon cushion. His right hand rests on his right knee, palm outwards. This is the mundra of giving. His left hand is in his lap and holds a bowl of medicines that can cure any illness.

4 Feel the compassion of the Medicine Buddha and ask in your heart that your illness may be taken away. Vow that you will use your health for the benefit of all sentient beings.

5 Now imagine that a beautiful beam of light is pouring down from above. It washes you clean as it passes over and through your body. See how the dark illness that you may see as black spots is washed away and replaced by brilliant light. Notice how you feel exhilarated and full of vitality. Your whole body is filled with crystal clear light.

6 Repeat the process a few times.

7 Now inwardly hear the mantra OM (pronounced AUM). It is coming from the Medicine Buddha and now fills the whole universe. Just like the light, the sound washes away your dark illness. With both the light and the sound, experience the divine love that showers all over and through you.

8 When you have finished rest a while. You may want to sleep. Allow the vibrations to quieten down before you resume your normal activities.

Chapter 9
What can the timeless wisdom of Tibet teach us about the wider environment and the purpose of human life?

The Tibetan Buddhists in exile and those who continue to practise their faith in occupied Tibet are an example to the world of altruism and compassion in the face of adversity. Nearly everything they cherish has been destroyed: their temples, literature, traditions; yet, despite this, the light of their teachings shines brighter than ever and is now a beacon to millions of spiritual seekers from around the world. At their heart lie the same essential teachings of all Buddhists as taught by Shakyamuni Buddha from India. Tibetan Buddhism is founded on the Four Noble Truths and the Noble Eightfold Path yet has evolved Shakyamuni Buddha's teachings to embrace the shamanistic religion of Bön. Today, the process of evolution continues and now absorbs and transforms Western ideas. From a feudal conservative society has sprung a religion that is liberal and flexible. Tibetan Buddhism flowered, seeded and now shaken by the iron fist of China has had its seeds scattered throughout the world.

One place where Tibetan Buddhism has taken root is in Scotland. In Edinburgh is the Tara College of Tibetan Medici~

in which the medical teachings are specifically designed to give a firm understanding of the philosophy and principles to Western students. Here, Eastern and Western medicine are practised side by side. Research is also considered an important aspect of their work and researchers are working on the translation and compilation of a comprehensive Materia Medica of Tibetan medicinal substances and the use of indigenous British plants. It has firm links with the Lhasa Mentzikhang, Tibet's central University of Medicine.

Scotland also has one of the world's centres of excellence for Tibetan Buddhism at Eskdalemuir in Dumfriesshire. Samye Ling was founded in 1967 and was the first Tibetan Centre in the West, taking its name from Samyey, the first Buddhist centre of learning in Tibet. Hundreds of people go there to stay, either attending courses or simply passing a private moment of reflection in this wild part of Scotland. Here, they believe that the central idea of Tibetan Buddhism is to improve the quality of every aspect of life by wisely applying the power of compassion. Their motto 'Helping where help is needed' expresses this ideal. The Samye is maintained by a community of 100 people and has a college, library, museum and a magnificent Shrine Room It is a place of deep spirituality and is the mother centre for its branch centres in Europe and Africa.

Of particular merit is its Holy Island Project. This island near the Isle of Arran in the West of Scotland is a natural haven of peace that has a long spiritual history and has rare flora and fauna. Since 1992 work has begun to create a Centre for Peace, Reconciliation and Retreat open to the people of all faiths. The Tibetans are also rebuilding the old Celtic chapel and extensive work is being done to re-forest sections of the island. As well as a place of retreat its objective is for it to 'become a model for harmony among peoples, and between humankind and nature'. Similarly, in the United States the Tibetan Plateau Project was established in 1992 to promote the conservation of medical plants and the environment. It is desperately under-funded.

Tibet was perhaps the first culture in the world to recognise the importance of looking after the environment. Their belief in the Buddhist teaching of Right Livelihood stresses the importance of 'contentment' and discourages greed, gluttony and over-consumption. The philosophy naturally frowns upon the over-exploitation of the Earth's natural resources. History's first environmentalist must have been the fifth Dalai Lama who, in 1642, issued a *Decree for the Protection of Animals and the Environment*. Since then, such decrees have been issued annually and today's Dalai Lama is an outspoken critic of governments that would destroy our world in the name of short-term profit. 'I have always believed the Earth is like our mother,' says the present-day incarnation of the Dalai Lama. 'Just as the Earth has given us life and sustained humanity through the ages, we have come to a stage where we need to look after this planet much more than we have been doing in the past.'

As the exiled Tibetans attempt to rebuild their culture and set an example of environmental management to the world, millions of ancient trees are being felled in Tibet. The country's rare flora is being rapidly destroyed and the rivers polluted by radioactive waste and toxic silt from the extensive Chinese mining projects. It is estimated that almost two-thirds of Tibet's forests have been destroyed since 1949. The damage is being increased further because of the huge influx of Chinese settlers into Tibet which is putting a tremendous strain on the delicate ecosystem. And, just like the American Indians, the Australian Aborigines and the Ancient Britons, the native Tibetans have become a minority in their own country.

The Tibetan Buddhists believe that material development is good for humankind but point out that spiritual development is also important for a good civilisation. Material development brings with it an increase in mental unease, worry and fear which may express itself in social discord and violence. There is also a greater degree of strife within the family and many unhappy separations.

The key to overcoming our problems lies within ourselves. Whether there are problems of economics, international relations, technology, ecology or whatever, there is always a human motivation at work. Reform the motivation and the world's problems are solved. Good motives will win through in the end. Also Tibetan Buddhism teaches us to not only use our head but use our heart as well. We must cultivate compassion, kindness and forgiveness. Without these qualities neither the individual nor society will ever know true peace. The Dalai Lama has stated that 'Only through inner peace can genuine world peace be achieved.' This must be created first within oneself, then in the family, then in the community, then in the nation and finally throughout the whole world.

The Tibetan teachings give the method to find this inner peace. This comes through compassion, love and respect for human beings. Tibetan Buddhism teaches us to become better people. This requires an attitude of service and refraining from doing harm to others– ethics which lie at the heart of all of the world's religions. Each religion has its own methods for achieving this goal and the goal of enlightenment, salvation, God consciousness or whatever term we may wish to use. Also each religion has its own doctrine and way of coming to the truth. For some, it is best to become Buddhists, others may prefer a Christian, Hindu, Jewish or Moslem path. A Tibetan would observe that what matters is not the outward display of faith but the intent and motive that makes a person strive towards greater spirituality. Whatever path you choose, take each step with love, transform intent into action, become the master of yourself, serve others and finally you will truly understand the purpose of human life.

When Gampopa asked the singing yogi Milarepa for his final spiritual instructions his reply was simple: 'What is needed is more *effort*, not more teachings'

He then remained silent but, as Gampopa crossed a narrow stream, Milarepa shouted to him from the other far bank 'Gampopa, I have one very profound secret instruction that is far too precious to give away to just anyone.'

Gampopa stood shocked as Milarepa pulled up his white robe and showed his buttocks. They were callused, hard skinned and pockmarked from year upon year of seated meditation on the cold rocks. 'That's my final instruction, heart-son!' came the voice that floated across the icy waters 'Do it!!!'[1]

[1] Story as told in *The Snow Lion's Turquiose Mane: Wisdom Tales from Tibet* by Lama Surya Das (Harper Collins)

Illustration

It is far to easy to fall into intellectual traps when you begin to study Tibetan Buddhism. There is a vast amount of literature already translated into Western dialects and no doubt more will become available to us as new texts are smuggled out of Tibet. It is easy to get swamped and lose sight of what is the essence of Tibetan wisdom so, if we want to gain anything from Tibet, we must start by putting our knowledge into practice. Only in this way does our understanding become wisdom. It is not the reading of sutras or the performance of rituals that's important, rather it is to live the truth we have heard. If we do this then we will see the Dharma in everything and in everyone. Everything we say and do, our duties at home, work and leisure, should be undertaken with the compassion that lies at its heart. In this way our feet will be in the world, but our mind will be high in the solitude of Tibet's holy mountains.

Application

Why not find out more by meeting real Tibetan lamas and helping Tibet to gain religious freedom and political independence? The following contact numbers and website addresses will enable you to find out more and help you to apply Tibetan teachings to your life.

Tibet Information Network – a non-political information and news agency giving detailed information about the Tibetan country and its people.
City Cloisters, 188–196 Old Street, London EC1V 9FR.
Tel: +44 (0)171 814 9011
http://www.tibetinfo.net

Free Tibet Campaign – Political pressure group to free Tibet from Chinese occupation.
1 Rosoman Place, London EC1R 0JY.
Tel: +44 (0)171 833 9958
http://www.freetibet.org/ict

International Campaign for Tibet – American organisation to free Tibet.
1825 K Street, NW Suite, 520 Washington DC 20006, USA.
Tel: +01 202 7851515
http://www.peacenet.org

The Tibet Foundation – Will help you find information about Tibetan Buddhism.
Can also advise where to find a teacher or meditation group in your area.
10 Bloomsbury Way, London WC1A 2SH.
Tel: +44 (0)171 404 2889
http://www.gn.apc.org/tibetgetza

The Tibet Fund – Affiliated to the Office of Tibet this organisation will help you find out all you need to know about Tibetan Buddhism or visiting Tibet.
241 East 32nd Street, NY 10016, USA.
Tel: +01 212 213 5011
http://www.tibetfund.org

Psychic Encounters – The author's website has information about Tibetan Buddhism, Spiritualism, Hinduism and has many more illustrations and applications that you can try.
http://www.psychics.co.uk

FURTHER READING

There are many thousands of books about Tibet and its religions. Here are a few of the modern and easy-to-understand books that have inspired me:

Burang, Theodore, *The Tibetan Art of Healing*, Robinson & Watkins Books, 1974
Chih-i, *Stopping and Seeing*, Shambhala Publications, 1997
Conze, Edward, *The Diamond Sutra and the Heart Sutra*, George Allen & Unwin Ltd, 1958
Dresser, Marianne, *Buddhist Women on the Edge*, North Atlantic Books, 1996
David-Neel, Alexandra, *Magic and Mystery in Tibet*, HarperCollins, 1967
David-Neel, Alexandra, *Initiations and Initiates in Tibet*, Rider & Company, 1931
Donden, Yeshi, *Health Through Balance: An Introduction to Tibetan Medicine*, Snow Lion Publications, 1986
Evans-Wentz, *Tibetan Yoga and Secret Doctrines*, Oxford University Press, 1934
Fremantle, Francesca and Trungpa, Chögyam, *The Tibetan Book of the Dead*, Shambhala, 1987
Gold, Peter, *Tibetan Pilgrimage*, Snow Lion Publications, 1998
Govinda, Lama Anagarika, *The Way of the White Cloud*, Rider, 1966
Guenther V. Herbert, *Treasures on the Tibetan Middle Way*, Shambhala, 1969
Hamilton-Parker, Craig, *The Psychic Workbook*, Ebury/Random, 1995
Hamilton-Parker, Craig, *Your Psychic Powers – a beginner's guide*, Hodder & Stoughton, 1996

Hamilton-Parker, Craig, *The Psychic Casebook*, Blandford/Cassell, 1999

Hamilton-Parker, Craig, *The Hidden Meaning of Dreams*, Sterling, 1999

Hess, Herman, *Siddhartha*, Picador, 1954

Kelder, Peter, *Tibetan Secrets of Youth and Vitality*, Thorsons, 1988

Lama, Dalai, *Awakening the Mind, Lightening the Heart*, Thorsons/HarperCollins, 1995

Lama, Dalai, *Kindness, Clarity and Insight*, Snow Lion Publications, 1984

Lhalungpa, Lobsang P, *The Life of Milarepa*, Paladin, 1997

Rinpoche, Akong Tulku, *Taming the Tiger*, Ebury Press, 1994

Rinpoche, Sogyal, *The Tibetan Book of Living and Dying*, HarperCollins, 1992

Sangharakshita, *The Buddha's Victory*, Windhorse, 1991

Thurman, Robert A. F., *Essential Tibetan Buddhism*, HarperCollins, 1995

Trungpa, Chögyam, *Cutting through Spiritual Materialism*, Shambhala, 1973

Tsarong, T. J. *Fundamentals of Tibetan Medicine*, Tibetan Medical Centre, 1981

Yeshe, Lama and Rinpoche, Zopa, *Wisdom Energy*, Wisdom Publications, 1976